THE
CARE AND CULTIVATION
OF INDOOR PLANTS

The
Care and Cultivation
of Indoor Plants

*

VIOLET STEVENSON

ODHAMS BOOKS

LONDON - NEW YORK - SYDNEY - TORONTO

Dedicated to

H. A. HAMILTON

First Published 1958
Seventh Reprint October, 1968
for Odhams Books by
The Hamlyn Publishing Group Ltd
Hamlyn House, 42 *The Centre*
Feltham, Middlesex

T.1068. R7.

PRINTED IN GREAT BRITAIN BY
JOHN GARDNER (PRINTERS) LTD.,
LIVERPOOL, 20

CONTENTS

ILLUSTRATIONS

CHAPTER ONE

SHAPE, FOLIAGE, FLOWERS
OR TEXTURE

SOME time ago I was asked for a definition of a house plant. It was required for the schedule of a flower show and was supposed to be both as concise and as accurate as possible so that there could be no misunderstanding. I replied in more or less these words: "A house plant is one that is grown indoors under normal living conditions and for periods of a year or more because of the beauty of its shape, its foliage, its flowers or its texture."

The man who asked me, a nurseryman-florist of international standing, appeared to be satisfied, so perhaps we may also adopt this as our own definition.

The important point is the implication of the words, "indoors under normal living conditions," for this is the boundary, the strict dividing line that immediately cuts some plants off and refuses them admission. The point is that where a Christmas tree or a pansy may be dug up and brought indoors, they will appear to grow for a limited period, but their life will depend entirely on the time they take to die. House plants are supposed to have a life of several years.

The growth of interest in home decoration by means of green plants has been striking in the past ten years. Flowering plants have been popular in the home for even longer. This awakened interest is largely architect inspired. The clear cut lines, sculpted forms and graceful habit of so many house plants have fitted modern furniture and decorative schemes. Some, again, have had that fashionable look, slightly bizarre,

9

almost amusing but with a touch of the practical. Modern and efficient heating systems have been unkind to cut flowers, which last a few days only. Plants, living a long time in comparison, can be fitted more closely into decorative schemes, used to trail or to climb, to reveal, accentuate or hide a feature of interior decoration.

Although the vogue for plants may strike us as a modern trend, it is really more of a revival or an adaptation than a new craze. Plants have always been grown in pots and indoors. And it was as recently as Victorian days that the fashion was at its latest peak.

Is it, I wonder, a mere coincidence that certain aspects of Victorian dress are now popular among both ladies and gentlemen? It is certainly interesting to note that with the exception of the *Ficus elastica*, the India Rubber plant, (in one Victorian gardening journal there is a reference to its ubiquity) the "Victorian" plants have been the last to be taken over by the home decorator. Thus we may deduce, if we are historical detectives, that Victorian fashions have not so much returned to us as have been adapted and altered to suit our more streamlined approach to life.

The Aspidistra, or cast-iron plant, that toughest of all indoor plants, is now coming on the scene again and one can expect to see more and more of it. I think it a handsome plant and that the variegated specimen is beautiful. In my jade green, cone shaped, tripod container, though, the plant certainly has nothing of the Victorian about it. The dracaenas and the palms are also once again finding their admirers.

Although plants were certainly popular in the last century, it was a physical impossibility that they could be as popular as they are now, for their houses were both colder and darker. Consequently only plants really difficult to kill, plants like the aspidistra, achieved real success.

On the other hand in those days the middle class were

wealthy by present day standards and could afford the luxury of a stove house in which to grow the plants that could be brought into the living quarters for a few days and then returned to recuperate under the care of a skilled and comparatively ill-paid gardener. These stove houses were fabulous things. Often adjoining the living quarters, they could be entered through french-doors. They were kept, in all seasons, at a temperature of 75 degrees or so and with a very high humidity, gained through constant watering of pathways and spraying of plants and air. They are not to be confused with the conservatory, which, although on much the same principle, was both cooler and less humid. The stove house could, of course, be used to grow the most tropical of plants and those of you who know some of the tropical houses at Kew will appreciate the sort of atmosphere that was obtained.

With what they could grow in their stove houses and with the palms and hortensias (hydrangeas) they could hire cheaply from a local florist, the Victorian paterfamilias decorated his house when holding a ball. The plants were as much a decoration as was then thought suitable and in good taste. The important thing was that the plants could be returned either to stove house or to florist the next day and there they would be able to recover from the frightful ordeal they had been through.

Yet, through breeding and through conditioning, many of the plants that were then suitable only for the stove houses are now growing in our homes in temperatures considerably lower and in humidities Sahara-like in comparison. Pay tribute, then, to the growers and hybridizers who have made possible this modern miracle.

Don't make the mistake of thinking that your plants are grown at the nursery under these conditions. Modern methods, modern greenhouses and modern heating mean that it is no longer necessary to grow them under extreme conditions of heat and humidity, yet the houses in which your plants are propagated and grown are both warmer and moister than any of our homes.

Some plants are grown from seed, but the majority come from cuttings taken off a parent plant. Most of us can take cuttings ourselves if we wish to. There's nothing secret or even particularly difficult about it. On the nursery they are able to give the germinating seed or the fresh cuttings just the care and the attention that they need and their proportion of losses is greatly below ours. Obviously this must be so, or they would not be able to make a living.

Scrupulous cleanliness, plenty of light and air, are just as essential as warmth and humidity. Even the water which moistens them is kept in huge tanks inside the houses so that it is always at a comfortable, even temperature.

Soil mixtures sometimes vary for different plants. We can understand that a bog plant like a cyperus will require a different soil from a dry semi-succulent like a sansevieria. Yet there is a standard soil compost.

So far as we are concerned, if we wish to take some cuttings, or if we wish to re-pot a plant that has grown too large for its present home, then we have the ready-made standard recipes prepared for us by the John Innes Horticultural Institution. The John Innes composts (of which more later) are obtainable from most garden stores and are wonderful for our purpose.

Some of the nurserymen use these, others have their own pet composts which they feel can be varied to give the particular requirements of the differing groups of plants. Whatever soil mixtures they use, they insist that their soils are sterilized. This means that all weed seeds are killed. Obviously if you are growing a new and precious plant from seed, you wish to know when you see a tiny shoot rise from the soil that this *is* your plant and not a weed that has germinated at the same time. So if possible, always use sterilized John Innes compost when you plant your cuttings. You will find it well worth while and you will be able to buy quite small quantities for only a very few shillings. Don't keep this compost for too long. If you do not use it all for your present purpose, then throw it on the garden, where it is bound to do good, and buy fresh when you want some more.

Really, you know, there's no need to worry much about soils unless you have had some plants for a year or so or unless you wish to go in for propagating in a big way. For all the plants that the nurserymen send out are in soil that will provide sufficient nourishment for the plants for anything up to a year. The plants don't even need much feeding in this time, for the soil that they are grown in is specially selected with all this in mind.

It is helpful, though, to know something of the root system, so that you can take a more intelligent interest in what is going on while your plants grow and develop in your home. Roughly speaking, most plants have a root system equal in size to the portion above the soil. I remember, years ago, seeing an exhibit at an agricultural show, where a mature tree was lifted in the air and all its roots were spread out above the ground. It was fascinating to see that the area occupied by the roots mirrored almost exactly the area of the branches.

Of course in a pot this just isn't possible. The roots can't spread like this because there isn't room. So instead they reach out while the plant is very young and after a time they come to the side of the pot. Then they begin to curl around this. After a time the roots form a thick layer, almost like pastry, around the sides of the pot. And curiously enough, when a plant has grown in its original pot like this for some time, you can knock it out and loosen the roots and find that there is hardly any soil left at all. That is why and when a plant needs re-potting. On the other hand, the soil is only a medium to hold and feed the plant. The pot holds it all right, so if you feed it regularly the plant will live (though it may not flourish as it should), almost indefinitely.

Elsewhere in these pages you will see a reference to a plant which I have had for seven years growing in the same pot. Just out of curiosity I have often wished to knock it out of its pot to have a look at the roots, but I am sure my curiosity will do it no good, so I leave it alone. It grows and it flourishes, but I know perfectly well that it would do better if I re-potted it with fresh soil. I wish merely to experiment. The leaves are smaller than they should be and it isn't as attractive as it could be. But this is just one example of what a plant will put up with if you make it. I doubt whether many plants would put up with this sort of treatment. But this one is a *Rhoicissus rhomboidea*, a grape-vine ivy, one of the hardiest and toughest of our house plants. In our home, for some reason, it has come to be known as Old Glory.

Needless to say, a plant cannot continue indefinitely in a pot, regardless of how much you feed it. For after a time the roots strangle each other. This is the main difference between a plant in a pot and one in the garden soil, for the latter has so much more room to spread its roots and, at the same time, a far greater area available to it for the seeking and absorption both of food and drink.

Just as more pot plants are killed by overwatering than any other cause, so many of them are killed by overfeeding. We must try always to remember that to a plant in a pot life is lived at an exaggerated rate. Everything is more concentrated— the space for its foliage, the room for its roots, its rate of respiration, its warmth, its feeding and its watering. We must take these things into account and when we feed a plant we should do so carefully, for too much food is just as bad for a plant as it is for a human being. Where we can resort to an indigestion cure, the plant must sweat out its bellyache. It has only two alternatives in its existence—life or death. The border between the two is a narrow one.

Again, in connection with both watering and feeding we

must always bear in mind the time of year. To plants indoors the seasons may not seem to matter so much, for they are protected against both extreme cold and extreme heat and live their lives in a comparatively artificial level atmosphere. Yet the life of all plants, indeed, of all living things, is based on a cyclic pattern of ebb and flow and regardless of the apparent artificiality of its surroundings, winter and summer are definitely vital to it. Summer is a time of growth and winter provides the time when the plant can rest, recover and gather strength for the next burst of energy.

Because our plants do not lose all their leaves in winter as do the trees, we are apt to forget the importance of winter as a dormant period. The leaves stay on the plant and there may even be a noticeable amount of growth. But the plant desperately needs a rest and to try to force it to grow and develop by means of watering and feeding is to tax the plant beyond its strength.

I get a considerable amount of correspondence from enthusiasts who ask my advice in one way or another. I have noticed frequently that during winter I get letters from people who are worried because their plants are losing leaves. Almost invariably it appears that watering is being continued at the summer rate and perhaps the plants are even being fed at the normal summer rate. Naturally, this is more than the plant can stand and to give evidence of its ill health it begins to drop its leaves. Food and water have to be balanced with the rate of growth.

One often reads that no food should be given to plants during winter as it is then that they rest, but I feel that this statement needs qualifying. We have to remember that our plants have originated in all parts of the world, yet they continue to flower in their own season.

Many plants such as azaleas, primulas, and cyclamen will be in full bloom in winter. Obviously since these *are* in bloom they are at the peak of their existence. In no way could they be termed as resting. Some "green" plants such as cyperus, the umbrella plant, or spathiphyllum will also be carrying flowers though if you have not a great deal of botanical experience you might not recognize those of the cyperus as such, for they will be green like the leaves of the plant. But flowers they are and a flowering plant cannot be a resting plant. In fact the very act of flowering often draws on its reserves so much that one must give extra food at this time rather than withhold it.

Much too depends upon the temperature and the amount of daylight during the winter months. Sometimes January and February are comparatively mild and there is no halt to growth. One finds that the plant is continually putting out new leaves or new shoots. Obviously it cannot be resting. Yet a few foggy days will often have an adverse effect which will be noticeable for days afterwards.

As a general rule continue to feed plants which are in flower and which are sending out young growth. But remember, should the season be severe and should they become influenced by the cold and dark (and this does not always follow if for example the plant is in a well lighted warm room), then take greater care over watering and withhold food until it is obvious that growth is active once again.

It might be well here, perhaps, to point out a little matter of psychology which, though obvious, is easily forgotten. Those of us who are gardeners have under our care a total of very many plants, trees, shrubs. There are so many, in fact, that simply because of their number and the area they occupy, no one plant claims your individual attention to the degree that you count the number of leaves that fall or watch the angle at which they droop. Yet indoors, simply because they are isolated, our plants gain the most concentrated attention. It is probably true to say that just as an only child is apt to be spoilt because it is the sole object of his parents' affection and attention, so many indoor plants are spoilt and coddled for the same

Left: Many plants can flourish away from the window. Here a green ivy *Hedera helix* is set on the shady side with *H. canariensis* nearer the light of the window.

Below: The same variety set to receive light from a standard lamp. Artificial light is good for plants unless they are set too close, where they may burn. On the right nearer the window, is a holly ivy, *H. cristata.*

Above: On the mantelshelf a copper wine bottle holder hides small pots (sixties) of (l. to r.) *Cissus striata, C. antarctica* and *Plectranthus oertandahlii.* Tradescantia tumbles over the edge in front.

Below: This trough at right angles to the window, holds a sansevieria nearest the light and a monstera away from the glare of the sun.

Left: Even large plants will grow in a small bowl if the plant food in the soil is well balanced.

Right: Mixed plants can serve many purposes: here a bowl of them has been latticed with a cane framework to look well against a wall.
Below: A plectranthus will trail effectively if given a little hidden support.

Left: Mixed plants are used below eye-level to decorate a low coffee table.

Below: The tureen holds a layer of drainage material and contains varieties of succulents which are most effective grown together.

reason. Although I do not advocate a deliberate policy of neglect, I do think that many of us (yes, I include myself) should strive to maintain a sense of proportion.

At the moment, in a corner of a wide shelf in front of a window in the kitchen, I have a *Hedera helix Chicago*. I have a rather particular affection for this plant as for many months it performed a useful service for me. It was down at our cottage in the country and it hid with a lush and magnificent display of foliage a rather shabby corner of our living room. This corner is comparatively dark but the ivy flourished and I was grateful. But because petrol was rationed and we couldn't get to the cottage as often as we would like, we brought most of our plants to London.

This ivy hated the move, as, in fact, we all did. It shed its leaves. I began to despair until common sense took over again. So I left it alone, giving it merely normal winter waterings, and of course new shoots, fresh green leaves and an atmosphere of life are once again appearing. I am sure that if I had continued to fuss, if I had moved it from place to place trying to find a home it liked, if I had dosed or amputated, then I should have killed it completely. On the other hand there are seasons when a severe pruning is beneficial as you can learn in a later chapter in this book.

No plant, indoors or outdoors, likes to be moved about too much. We all feel happiest in comfortable, familiar surroundings and are unhappy when forced to move. A plant is just the same. So long as its position is not draughty, not too near direct heat, so long as it has a source of light, then leave it there, or if you must move it, do so as seldom as possible.

Plants may, of course, be moved about within the orbit of their accustomed positions. In fact this is very necessary. For a plant that has been in one spot for more than a few days will naturally turn its leaves to the light and should be moved constantly on its axis to prevent malformation. There are times though when we can use this characteristic to decorative effect —when for example, the plant grows on a wall opposite a window—but more of this later.

It is not necessary for plants to be right in the window. In fact this is not really a good position, for some draughts are certain to get through and such a position is apt to be both too hot in summer and too cold in winter. The most suitable situation for the average home in Britain is fairly near a good window, and which aspect is chosen will depend to a certain degree on the plant. Some demand good light, others show a surprising tolerance of shade. On the whole we can generalize and say that flowering plants and those with coloured foliage are better with plenty of light, although direct sunlight must be used with caution. Plants with heavy, dark leaves can do with less light.

Nearly all plants, if natural light from a good window be difficult, will gain from artificial light. Care must be taken that the light is not too hot for them however, for electric bulbs give off a surprising amount of heat. There are, I regret to say, a number of light fitments on the market which incorporate special stands for plants. These should be viewed with the utmost suspicion, for in most cases any plant placed in them will be scorched, sometimes fatally.

Many growers make use of artificial light for various reasons into which I need not go now, and a number of plants, including saintpaulias or African violets in particular, have been grown very successfully in this country with no light whatsoever other than artificial light.

Luckily, signs that a plant is not getting enough light are easy enough to detect. The leaves lose colour, yellowing and becoming almost transparent. Growth becomes weak, long and spindly. (This is nature's way of reacting to a shortage of light, for this stimulates the growth cells to push the plant upwards towards the source of light.)

I have used the analogy before, but it bears repeating: treat your plants as though they are pets. Give them food, water, light and warmth. Protect them from draughts. Let them get used to their home and give them the comfort and security of a settled position.

The analogy fails in one respect. If a pet is given food or water it will eat and drink its fill. If it wants more it will soon let you know. If it has too much it will leave its saucer and come back later. But you yourself have to make the decision for your plants and your decisions mean the difference between healthy long life and speedy unhappy death. So get to know your plants, discover which like watering frequently, which seldom. The instructions you may receive with your plants or the books such as this that you open for your guidance, can give you only rough guidance, for so much depends on the atmosphere of your home, its temperature and light, even on the locality in which you live.

So never obey blindly and to the letter any directions you may be given. Take them for guidance only and watch carefully how your plant reacts. After a little practice you will soon learn whether more or less water is required, whether the light is sufficient for the plant, whether it requires feeding or re-potting. If you treat your plant as it likes to be treated it will repay you a thousandfold.

CHAPTER TWO

GETTING TO KNOW THEM

WITHOUT going to sentimental extremes it is true to say that plants can engage your affections. You have them long enough for them to attain personality and individuality, for you to recognize when they look healthy or when they are sickening. This has its drawbacks as well as its advantages, for although later on we shall be discussing "temporary" and "permanent" plants, let us face the fact that there is no such thing as a truly permanent plant indoors unless perhaps the aspidistra qualifies. Some will last for years and will apparently flourish and suddenly, due perhaps to negligence, accident and mistaken zeal, they will die. There are too, plants which will give us great pleasure for a few weeks and then like old soldiers—simply fade away. By using tremendous effort and ingenuity, by transferring them to garden or glass house and then back indoors again, by coddling and nursing, we may keep them alive. But is it worth it? They will never regain the splendour of their prime. Far better, I think, to treat them as you would a bunch of cut flowers. Enjoy them to their utmost while they are at their best and then, with gratitude, discard them.

This advice will perhaps go against the grain to some. The ailing plant will be a challenge, and how good that it should be so! I would be the last to discourage such an attitude, for among the very many plants that decorate our flat in London and our home in the country some have been near death on more than one occasion and have been nursed back to health again. It is true, I believe, to say that every time a plant has faltered it has been due to human cause and not to any inherent weakness or disease of the plant itself.

Perhaps I have been away longer than expected and the pot was not watered. Perhaps it was watered both by me and my husband or left carelessly in the draught from an open window or too near to a fire or not moved far enough away when the decorators invaded! Unless these errors are left too long before being rectified little permanent damage is done.

Certainly there is enjoyment to be gained in observing the condition of one's plants, in watching their growth and development, catching the fall of a leaf or the yellowing of foliage in time to take careful action.

Lest the first few lines in this book may give the impression that house plants are always ailing and must be tended and guarded with care, may I reassure you by saying that this is not so. In the past five years or so I must have had at least a hundred house plants. Some I still have. One old warrior, Old Glory, I have had in two homes for seven years. It still occupies the same pot in which it was grown. Although some plants have died, their death has been occasioned by deliberate experiment to see just what punishment they would take or by the fierce lights of floodlamps so that they could be photographed. At the moment I have plants in every room, including bathroom and lavatory! I have green plants and flowering plants, bulbs in bowls and cacti and succulents in pots.

So far as my memory serves me there are, in fact, just under fifty plants at present in my small London flat. This may seem to be a large number yet I assure you that we are not overcrowded nor hemmed in by plants. We do not feel we must use a machete to get to the bedroom nor need we peer through curtains of ivy to see whether it is raining.

London is a dark, dirty, dusty city and for this reason all the plants we have here would soon become covered in time with a fine coat of dirt and dust. So elaborate plant decorations involving training shoots to grow over walls are impractical, for the leaves collect the dust and transfer it to the walls. The foliage also demands regular cleaning if the plant is to continue in good health. So most of our plants are positioned for convenience as well as for decorative effect. With two homes and one each of husband and child, I am a busy woman and can spare little time to groom, feed, water and tend my plants. They must be subordinated to my way of life, not I to theirs. So the plants that occupy a permanent place in my homes and in my affections are those that give me most in return for the little I am able to give to them.

Indoor plants vary just as much as those which grow in the garden for there are herbaceous kinds, shrubs, trees, climbers and creepers, there are bulbs, tubers and corms. There are perennials, biennials and annuals and there are evergreens and deciduous plants. Just as when you are choosing plants for a garden you are influenced by the aspect, landscape, sun and shade so should you be guided by the character of your home.

Some people though don't plan to become plant fanciers but get pleasantly along the path of indoor gardening by the impetus of a gift. At Christmas or some other anniversary comes an azalea, an ivy, a solanum or a bowl of cactus. If the plants die quickly then often any interest that might have been kindled dies too. But should the happy recipient of the plant find that the care she has given her little plant has made it thrive then she becomes anxious to try her green fingers on some other, and so another gardener is born!

However if we are able to choose plants we ought to be influenced by the purpose they are to serve and by their ultimate position in the house. If it is colour we are after it might be that the flowering plants will serve us best. Although here I must say that many of the newer introductions of "permanent" house plants have wonderfully colourful leaves; these are described in detail later on.

Getting to Know Them

For the sake of convenience house plants are divided into two groups, temporary and permanent plants. The terms speak for themselves although "permanent" needs to be taken at its hairdresser's value! Generally speaking, the temporary plants may be considered to have a life, once brought indoors, which is measured in weeks while that of the permanent plants may be measured in months or even years. We should aim for years!

The temporary plants are better known than the "new" permanent kinds. Nearly every one of us has had one at some time or another. Most of them are old friends, homely plants that have been with us for generations, at least their tribes have, but nowadays we have the advantage of being able to buy the modern hybrids and varieties which have larger individual flowers and brighter colours than ever our grandmothers saw. Primulas are better now than when I was a girl and so are one of the few things in life that improve as the years pass instead of becoming more beautiful in retrospect!

In the next chapter, which deals with what to look for when buying plants, I discuss these temporary plants more fully but suffice it to say here that they include such flowering kinds as azaleas, cyclamen, heathers, primulas, cinerarias, genistas, crassulas, hydrangeas, the berried solanums and capsicums, and the ornamental leaved coleus. All of which have been grown with one aim; that they should be at their best when they reach the customer. It is never intended, I think I am right in claiming, that they should last for many months but rather that one should enjoy the flowering beauty of a plant that you yourself could not bring to perfection without a great deal of experience, labour and expense.

It is only natural that one should want the flowers to go on as long as possible. Yet what so often happens is that from the moment it comes into the home the flowers slowly but steadily decline in beauty and life. Some that have been wrongly treated go off immediately. I remember an uncomfortable afternoon I once spent in a New York centrally heated apartment watching a tiny azalea pinned high on the wall shrivelling before my eyes. I wanted desperately to do something about it, but I and my hosts had only just met and I realized that even if I did do anything at that time the situation would be the same on the next day.

As a rule the plants have been timed to be at the peak of perfection at their time of sale. The compost is rich and blended to supply the plant its needs. But if you had raised that plant from seed in your greenhouse you would continue to care for it even more at its flowering period. In some cases you would begin to give it a little richer food so that it should not quickly exhaust itself but continue to send up even more flowers. Yet what so often happens is that a plant in this condition is handed over to someone who has never had any kind of plant to care for before. How are they to be expected to know by instinct what a gardener has to be trained to expect?

If any plant indoors or out is faced with sure extermination there seems to be some acceleration in the living pattern—a rush to get things over and done with as it were. What you have to do is to extend some kind of calming influence. A good drink immediately it comes into your hands (unless you have been forewarned that this has just been given) to ensure that the plant is unlikely to flag by the next day. And from then on a pinch of plant food or a plant tablet regularly. Any fading flowers should be picked off so that the plant does not turn its attention to trying to seed instead of producing more flowers.

With some plants there will not be more flowers to come than you can see buds, these include azaleas, hydrangeas, genistas, cinerarias, but the wrong treatment will cause the buds never to mature—particularly if at some time the plant is allowed to get bone dry.

Others, though perennial in nature, will throw up flowering stalks not visible when they come to you. These include primulas, cyclamen, gloxinia, geraniums and saintpaulias. In fact with the correct treatment some of these may be kept for years and will need re-potting or even dividing like garden plants.

Although their lives are fleeting the temporary plants include some of the loveliest in the world. There is a richness and exotic flavour about them that is quite apart from any other form of house decoration. To many people they bring a touch of luxury and yet even though they are valued in one sense they are disregarded in another. Too often the plant is left to stand on its own merits. Nothing seems to be done to merge the plant in with its surroundings. It so often stands a thing apart almost saying—"Look at me, I'm a special pot plant."

This is particularly the case when the hue of the blooms is considered. Quite often, of course, the plant is a gift and one has no choice in the matter but I have known women and men too who go to infinite trouble to harmonize carpets, walls and curtains and then buy an azalea or hydrangea that has no relation to the colour scheme at all.

Perhaps it is the fault of the shop-keeper that they do so, not knowing that a good range of hues exists in nearly all flowering plants. Hydrangeas can be bought red as well as pink, violet blue as well as duck-egg. Some are white and some cream coloured. Azaleas, reminiscent perhaps of apple blossoms, come in terra-cotta, vivid magenta and amethyst. Primulas have left most of that fierce pink behind them and are in all hues of reds and as near blue as it is, so far, possible to get—and so it goes on. If you are set on a certain colour, worry it out, until you can discover if a plant is available in that particular hue. It might surprise you to find how often you can be satisfied.

Not only is the colour factor important. Surely the way a plant is staged is significant. How much lovelier a plant smothered with bloom is likely to look displayed in a well chosen vase which lifts up and delightfully displays its flowers as though it were a well contrived flower arrangement, than if it is merely stood pot uncovered in an old saucer. How much more effective too if three or four harmonizing plants are grouped together than if they are staggered out on the window-sill.

One of the most effective groups I have seen was a charming group of flowers, china and glass. In a large pink and white tureen was grouped a large matching pink cyclamen and three smaller cyclamen in different hues one of which was amethyst. This bowl stood before a large window. On the sill flanking the plant arrangement were two Victorian lustres in the same amethyst tint of the flowers. A lovely picture, and a fine example of imaginative use of plants.

Personally, I think that while one considers a plant only as a separate individual to be left to stand alone one is bound to remain fixed in one's conception of its decorative possibilities. But considered as a single ingredient in an arrangement of several items, temporary, permanent and even cut flowers combined, it takes on a new and more important role. For example, if you have visitors coming, your natural impulse is probably to buy flowers to decorate the house. If time is short and if you are likely to have a crowded schedule while your visitors are staying then one or two plant arrangements made from plants at hand might serve you much better for they can be quickly assembled and with little trouble. What one should realize is that they can be just as colourful and quite as interesting, if not more so on occasions, as a flower arrangement.

Permanent plants are what we would call if they grew in the garden (and some do) and for want of a better name, evergreens, although only about half of them are really green. More of them are likely to be speckled or banded in white, cream, primrose, yellow, amethyst, purple, rose, orange and grey. Quite often there will be more than one hue combined with green in a leaf. Some will have brightly coloured under surfaces others will have tips of contrasting hues. Some of them like clivias, anthuriums, begonias, and spathiphyllum will bear flowers and some of these will be showy too. Others bear flowers which are green and even freakish. They vary considerably in both habit and appearance but the important point and one they have in common is that there is not a seasonal leaf drop with them as there is with deciduous shrubs, trees and climbers.

Occasionally a leaf will drop when it has served its purpose and grown old in doing so but this should be a rare occurrence. Should there be excessive leaf fall then this should be taken as an indication that something is wrong either with the plant or the way it is being cared for.

The many climbers are fascinating and are most popular. There is something very attractive about the pattern of leaves against a wall or silhouetted against the light. It is a great joy to me in the country to wake and see on the outside of the window the pattern of oak and sycamore leaves against the changing sky. Here in London there would be none of this same anticipatory joy in waking if it were not for the plants near my window.

Suspended from the picture rail on an ingeniously fastened stick is Old Glory. At the side of it and growing taller every week is a syngonium, its aerial roots anchored in a length of cork bark which helps to support and succour it. Its leaves are almost identical with the arrow-shaped wild arum which grows in the hedgerows except that in this case they are on climbing stems.

Some of these plants are best allowed to trail as freely as they wish, others are better supported so that they appear to climb. Occasionally they can be so displayed that they do both. Old Glory is one in this category. It has long ago grown well above the height of the wicker champagne bottle which holds and conceals the pot. This has now been suspended on a thin strong string and attached to a support which can be bought from any florist very cheaply. It consists of a cream painted bar of strong wood attached to a picture rail hook. It hooks on very firmly and one can easily attach any kind of suspended holder to it. Some trails of the plant are encouraged to climb up this string. Meanwhile the lower shoots cascade out from the wicker mesh and well below the basket base.

You probably know well the Virginian creeper which sets the walls of cottages on fire with its vivid foliage in early autumn. There are some closely allied indoor plants of the same family and Old Glory, *Rhoicissus rhomboidea*, is one of them. Its common name is grape-vine ivy and I quote it as an example of how the homely names can confuse the uninitiated for although this plant is indeed distantly related to the grape it has no connection with ivy but has obviously been given this term simply because it trails.

Some people seem to believe that there is some kind of snobbery in using latin plant names but there really is a great deal of sense rather than nonsense in their use. The technical name is usually divided into two parts, very occasionally there are three. The first part of the name is the family name something like a surname. The second is the specific name and indicates any special characteristics. These are described by the name. For example in *Hedera helix*, the term *hedera* is the ivy's scientific name—there are many hedera among the house plants. The specific term *helix*, means "spiral, or to turn round spirally as ivy." As a point of interest the common snail is called *Helix helix*, because its shell is spiral, not as one might be forgiven for thinking because it eats ivy!

Some plants though have varied from their species and are called varieties. A homely example is the coloured poppies rising from the wild red field poppy called "Shirley poppies". The varietal name is usually anglicized. Thus you will find *Hedera helix Chicago* given to a small leaved much branched form of the common ivy.

We have many hedera and there follows in a later chapter more detailed descriptions about them. Grown naturally outdoors against a rough wall the ivy will push its aerial roots into any cracks it can find and so climb often covering the whole surface. When it reaches the top it will trail over and hang in a pretty frill of vegetation often along the whole length. Without the wall near it and the inducement to climb and to make provision for climbing the ivies will not send out aerial roots but will remain smooth stemmed and will spiral in the characteristic manner.

You can persuade certain other plants to climb an indoor wall too if it has a rough surface. Two of the ficus will do this very prettily. They are *Ficus pumila* and *Ficus radicans* which means incidentally "rooting, particularly of stems and leaves."

Not all permanent plants are climbers or trailers. Some are so erect that they resemble a small tree—which of course they would be if they were grown naturally. The "India Rubber" plant *Ficus elastica* is an example. Nowadays, *Ficus decora*, nearly related but hardier is sold more often. This plant has large leathery leaves. If you prefer a daintier foliage *Ficus benjamina* will suit your purpose. All sizes may be bought but those in large pots really are tree-like. The pointed, shiny green leaves much resemble those of a lemon tree. They are, and indeed the whole plant is, most attractive.

It is not always appreciated that the pot geranium is a shrub rather than a herbaceous plant. As a rule fresh cuttings are propagated each autumn so that there is always a sequence of young plants. However, you may if you wish (and if you can) grow the plant so that it is continuously potted on. I once saw a plant which covered the wall on one side of a lean-to conservatory. It had been trained and secured in place and was a riot of scarlet blooms.

Most of the other indoor plants are herbaceous though there are some with bulbous, or what are known as rhizomatic, roots.

These are thick and fleshy like horse-radish. The actual plants vary in shape from each other according to the character and mode of growth of the foliage. *Peperomia hederifolia* forms a round dome-like cluster but the dracaenas with long pointed leaves are fountain-like. There is so much variety in shape that there never can be monotony.

All the plants I mention in this book are obtainable. They can be ordered from any florist who is willing to sell them or from a nurseryman who specializes and who has a retail trade. However, there are some you might like to raise yourself. If you are a greenhouse gardener you will probably know of these already and will already grow or plan to grow, coleus, gloxinias, begonias, cyclamen, cinerarias and saintpaulias.

Even without a greenhouse there are a few "exotics" well worth trying even if it means going to a little extra trouble. These are climbing annuals. They may be grown up the side of a window or even used as a curtain to cover the panes should the glass be frosted or reeded or should there be an unpleasant or dull view beyond.

Germinate the seeds in a warm sunny window or in the airing cupboard (see that the soil never dries out and that the seedlings are brought out into the light as soon as they have germinated). Sow three seeds in a 48 pot in John Innes seed compost and pot on later in potting compost No. 2. It helps germination if a pane of glass or a top of polythene is put over the pot. This helps conserve moisture and prevent evaporation. Or you may like to be really up to date and sow the seeds in a ready-made "propagating frame" which consists of a plastic food box. Sift about an inch of moist soil on the floor of the box. Press it down to firm it a little, sprinkle or arrange (according to size) the seeds on it, sprinkle a very shallow covering over and replace the lid. Leave it on until the seeds have all germinated. Then prick them out one plant to a small 60 and then pot on when they are big enough.

If you are unable for some reason or another to raise these plants either ask a friend with a greenhouse to start them off for you, or arrange with a nurseryman to do so. Some nurserymen list the following plants I am to describe. On another page you will see illustrated a plant of *Cobea scandens* growing across a window in my little son's nursery. This was taken early in the summer so the plant is not yet in flower but *Cobea scandens* or the cup and saucer flower is a lovely thing indeed. The buds and young flowers are green and as they mature the trumpet-collared flowers, turn white or purple according to the variety.

The plant's rate of growth can be compared to the legendary beanstalk. Each day a few more inches of uncurling leaves and enchanting tendrils are to be seen. The great moment comes when the flower buds are visible. When at last the blooms actually open they take their time maturing. Each day there is a difference in colour or hue to wonder over. Even when they fade the "saucer" persists for some time. A few people are even lucky enough or clever enough to look after their plants so well that they are rewarded by exotic purple fruits. Incidentally *Cobea scandens* is a hardy climber which may be grown outside against the wall of a house.

Another climber I would warmly recommend is the wonderful blue convolvulus which Americans call the Morning Glory. Its technical name is *Ipomaea*. There are several species and varieties in more hues than blue. For indoors and for the most spectacular growths you need *Ipomaea* Heavenly Blue. It will give you more and larger flowers than the rest. We have had our slender vine covered with these intense blue trumpets on a summer's morning. They do not last the day out but there is always a queue of intricately whorled buds waiting their turn to flower and so create a succession of bloom.

Often in the following pages I shall stress the need for light to grow plants successfully. But there are a few that will grow well in dark corners. Not all of us have rooms that are continually flooded with day or sunlight. It seems to me too, that it is the dark corner that most needs a plant to bring it to life. A variegated aspidistra, its leaves kept so well washed and cared for that they have a gloss, will shine out in a way you may never have imagined—more so too if you raise it up in a white, yellow, pale green or shining metal container.

Scindapsus aureus hates direct sunlight and the best plant I ever saw outside a nursery was growing in a shop high on the wall which shut off the window from the rest of the shop. Here it received no direct daylight at all. The shop being in Covent Garden closed at four in the afternoon so even the hours when the lights were on were comparatively brief.

The *Ficus lyrata* or fiddle-leaf fig is another Jack Horner, but its leaves are dark green. Give it the compliment and complement too of a light wall as a background.

Many of the philodendrons, hederas, ferns and the sansevieria, even though this is a sun worshipper, will grow well back in a room or even a windowless hall where there is artificial light.

Plants used to screen a window can suggest a country atmosphere.
Long trails may be secured against the glass with adhesive tape.

In this sparsely furnished room the large ficus furnishes the farther corner while the room divider holds a collection of fatsias, begonias, coleus and succulents placed high for maximum light.

CHAPTER THREE

A WELCOME FOR YOUR PLANTS

I T IS probably safe to say that all of our indoors plants have
been grown under greenhouse conditions, warm, humid
and draught free. But only those that have a certain tolerance of other atmospheres are selected and put on the market
as indoor plants. Simply because the plant has been accepted
for domestic decoration however, we cannot subject it to the
same discomforts that we put up with ourselves in our British
homes. After all, we can grumble, huddle nearer the fire or
open the window if we feel like it. But the plant just has to take
it until it can do so no longer.

The four things that plants get in their early greenhouse days
that help them to grow and give them a good start in life are:
warmth, steady temperature and freedom from draughts, light
and humidity. Of these basic requirements of a healthy plant,
we are normally able to supply only warmth and light. For
indoors our temperatures fluctuate and however well built or
designed our homes we cannot avoid a certain amount of draught
through ill-fitting doors or windows, up or down chimneys or
even constantly opening and closing doors. Our temperatures,
generally speaking, rise to a peak in the evening and then
swiftly drop during the night. The air we breathe is harsh and
dry.

It's really surprising sometimes just what plants will put up
with and it is a great tribute to growers that most of the plants
we buy last as they do. We are lucky in Britain that we have
such a fine tradition of gardening, for this runs throughout the
nursery trade. If I may be personal for a minute, I would like

33

to say that I have always had the greatest admiration for the professional honesty of the many men and women who grow plants and flowers for our markets. It is rare indeed to find anyone who places shoddy goods before the public and if a grower should do this he gets a bad name among his fellows exceedingly swiftly.

Given this tradition of honest dealing, what are we to look for when we choose a plant? For we must remember that we seldom have an opportunity of buying direct from the nursery. Most of us who live in cities have to buy from a florist and this means that the plants have left the nursery, travelled to market and been sold there either by the grower's salesmen or by a wholesale florist. The retail florist just around your corner has to buy the plants from the market, transport them to his own establishment and there, finally, place them on show for your selection. Obviously there have been several opportunities for some harm to come to the plant and with the best will in the world it isn't always possible for the retail florist to keep a close enough eye on each of his many plants to ensure that they are always in the best of condition.

So far as plants which flower are concerned, our method of marketing means that there is unlikely to be sufficient time for any of the blooms to have passed their peak and be on the way out. Should you be offered any plant on which it is obvious that even one flower is fading treat it a little suspiciously and select another if you can. It may be that it has been hanging about a little too long since it left the nursery. The trouble is that although plants may suffer no ill from this, particularly if they have been in the care of someone who knows how to look after plants, too many of them do pick up minor complaints during a prolonged spell between leaving their original home and coming to yours. What the nurseryman likes to do is to cut that period to the minimum.

It is bad enough for the plant to suffer shock and have to

34

adjust itself to the atmosphere of your home but if it also has had to adjust itself to market and shop as well, events might prove too much for it. Unfortunately effects may not show until it has been with you for a week or two.

So watch out for fading blooms. Examine the plant too to make sure that the flowers are not flagging. This may be caused only through thirst and is something soon rectified, but flagging can also be caused through draughts and severe cold. My guide is to buy plants and flowers rather in the same way as one chooses salad vegetables. Look primarily for crispness and colour. Whether the plant you seek bears flowers or whether it is grown for the beauty of its foliage, a healthy plant has a certain crisp appearance about it. Stems are turgid, stiff, not limp or drooping. Colour should be deep and glowing rather than semi-faded and transparent. Certain leaves have a metallic sheen on them which is more intensified when they are in the pink of condition.

Accept nothing that has spots on it, that is, spots which are obviously the result of burning or disease. The tissues of these spots will be drier than the main leaf fabric or blistery in appearance. Some green plants have a slight deposit caused from the water with which they have been sprayed, particularly if it is limy, but this is easily smoothed away and does no damage. The florist usually washes, and so polishes, the leaves before the plant is put on sale. Should the leaf be spotted, to test merely wipe the leaf gently between the finger and thumb and the misty appearance should disappear.

Some leaves may appear to have a dried brown edging to them. Do not accept a young plant in a small pot in this condition for this is usually the indication of a damaged or sick leaf. However, should the plant be a handsome specimen with very many leaves, begonias are examples, it might be that one or two of the older, that is the first formed leaves, are on their way out, as might be expected. They still have a role to play for leaves are the lungs of a plant, its stomach too for that matter, and it is unwise to cut away any leaf while it still has life for it continues to contribute to the well being of the plant and is part of its metabolism.

Examine the growing tips or shoots to make sure that they are sturdy, healthy and capable of further growth. Buds should be succulent. Pointed tips as in philodendrons should be well filled and plump. If they are papery they probably do not contain a living shoot.

If you are looking at a flowering plant, make sure that many buds are on the plant and that they seem capable of opening to bring you the joy of further brilliant flowers as the plant develops.

Whether the plant is temporary or permanent always treat yellowing leaves with suspicion, unless, of course they are supposed to have some yellow variation in them. One finds that if a leaf of a green plant yellows because of ill health there is usually some change of texture too. It becomes less tough, sometimes even pappy to the touch. Several yellowing leaves on ivy, cyclamen, hydrangea or bulb flowers usually indicate that the plants are older than they ought to be or very sick, though one leaf may, as I have suggested, merely be a spent leaf and is no cause for worry.

Growers of all kinds of plants, not only those used for home decoration, take great pride in producing specimens that retain their foliage. Stark, bare bases to stems, speaking generally, are not approved, for the plant can always use, and indeed needs, all the leaves it can produce. The same applies to plants you buy. Unless the stems are naturally leafless, such as the cyperus which produces little umbrella like topknots, the foliage should persist to the base. This need not necessarily be thick and bushy but it should be healthy and these leaves will obviously be older than those at the tip.

Since we buy most plants for the beauty of their leaves, and since the shape, texture and habit of leaf is characteristic of each species or variety of plant, we should study them carefully for they are one of the many faces of a plant. The ability to recognize at one glance at its leaves whether a plant is sick, overfed, smothered or overwatered comes only with experience and with much handling of plants. With experience comes the sensitivity that produces a good gardener.

Plants like solanums, or winter cherries as they are sometimes called, heaths and azaleas, all entirely different kinds of plants, show that they are unhappy about something by shedding their leaves. One or two only may drop but sometimes these one or two are the beginning of a real fall.

If when you go to buy a plant, on the soil surface you see a leaf or, in the case of heathers, some "needles," do not buy the plant, unless its length of life is really of no consequence.

Some plants are more subject to pests than others. You can all unwittingly bring an infected plant into the home and so infect others. Nothing like so many though come to market these days now that growers have access to such a wide range of more effective insecticides. However, it is a wise precaution if you have reason to doubt to inspect *under* the leaves of some plants. Cinerarias are subject to aphis attacks. On an infected plant you will see clusters of still, almost lifeless tiny insects.

The evergreen permanent plants do not appear to suffer from much at all, at least that is my experience. A scale insect sometimes infects hedera, staghorn fern and orchids. We found that we inadvertently brought home scale on a plant bought from a different source than usual. Subsequently we had to examine all our plants, but only the ivies succumbed, and these were soon free from infection.

Should you find a plant contaminated you will learn how to deal with the offenders in Chapter Seven.

In the summer of 1956 we suffered an invasion of caterpillar. Unseen by us these had hatched out and were well tucked in to tradescantia, coleus and young ivy leaves before we were aware of what had happened. Subsequently we found no less than three large brown moths, whose wings were orange when expanded, inhabiting our rooms. How they found their way into a room in Central London is a mystery, but they certainly wreaked havoc. We later found that they had also left their offspring on plants on the roof garden. As these had been cottoned to keep off the sparrows the caterpillars had been having a grand beano. I hate killing things but any moth seen now has to be exterminated.

In spite of the formidable lists of plant pests and diseases one can find in books which deal with the subject I would say that more plants die of thirst and drowning than anything else. Drowning is caused by overwatering and is forgivable. Correct watering is something that has to be learned but allowing a plant to die of thirst is unforgivable.

Right from the very beginning one has to realize that plants are living things. Like ourselves most of them can get along without food for a long time but they can remain alive only a few days without water.

As soon as you get a plant home, or as soon as one is delivered to you give it a drink. Take a bucket or bowl or if you have several plants use the sink, but see that the water level will come above the rim of the pot. Plunge the pot in carefully and watch for a stream of bubbles which should rise from the soil to the surface of the water. Wait until the stream of bubbles stops. Take out the pot plant and stand it on the draining board or in the sink, wherever you will and scrub the outside of the pot with clean tepid water. If the plant is the kind that will appreciate it spray its leaves also with clean tepid water. Stand it on a newspaper to drip and drain.

By all means buy a plant that appeals to you when you see it even though you know little of its habits or history but do not forget that you can order a particular plant. Not only can you state what kind of plant you want, but also its variety and size. You should be able too to determine the price beforehand.

The most popular size of pot plant is a 60 or three inch, measured across the rim, but there is a large 60 and a small 60. Take care when buying containers that this is taken into account or you will be left with a misfit. After this comes the 48. Pots came by these odd terms because of the way they are made—the 3 inch and 3½ inch are or were originally manufactured in casts of 60, the 5 inch pot in casts of 48, the 6 inch in casts of 32 and so on to the really large individuals. As I have said earlier I prefer to buy a 48 simply because the plant can remain established in this larger pot so much longer than in a 60. This is an infant pot (although "thumbs" are even smaller) and although we need not be in a hurry to re-pot our new plants it stands to reason that a plant which thrives is soon going to be too restricted in a very small pot. We find too that small pots are apt to dry out rather quickly once they carry a lot of growth. A plant in a 48 is usually about twice the price of the same plant in a 60.

Sometimes I am asked what I consider to be the best buys in plants. Like so many things it all depends on how you wish to use them and, more important still on your individual tastes. I like so much to see a plant bursting with good health that I am not very sympathetic to those people who try to drag a plant on month after month or year after year when it is only too obvious that it would like to die in peace and be consigned back to the good earth whence it sprung.

I have kept azaleas and cyclamen and have been rewarded but unless you have had some experience the results can be most disappointing. My advice, given earlier I know, is to treat these flowering plants as you would a bunch of flowers. Enjoy them while they are at their best and then wish them good-bye.

There are a few, like the hydrangea, rhododendron and *Primula kewensis* or even the solanum if you live in Cornwall or the Channel Isles, which may be planted out in the garden when you have done with them indoors. And of course all bulbs may be planted from bowl or pot to garden border. If they have been forced they may not bloom the first year after planting.

Although those plants mentioned above are perennial they do not behave as perennials should if left in their pots unless you are a skilled gardener and appreciate their demands. By this I mean that it is not easy to give them the correct conditions, food and treatment that would result in another equally good crop of flowers the following season.

However, one of the primulas, *obconica*, is a good pot perennial. Given plenty of stimulants and water the plant will grow and bloom until often it has to be divided or re-potted. The pretty red balsam is another old faithful. The "lily" types of plants such as clivias, agapanthus and Jersey Lily are all perennials. The other pot primula, *sinensis*, is not so obliging and in spite of its glorious colours not quite such a good buy being a little more difficult to look after.

I would always buy an azalea on the least provocation. Mainly I think because we have nothing else quite like them. They are such exotics. They are, too, well worth the money charged for them so long as they are properly cared for. But they should *never* be allowed to become dry. Once the petals flag—and they often flop together when this happens—they never look as fresh and as springlike again even though they do become turgid again after being stood in water. Often flagged petals become browned.

If you wish to try to grow the azalea on for another year, wait until the frosts are all over and then bury the pot in the garden up to its rim. Choose a shady place where the plant is not likely to be baked by the summer sun. Never let the plant dry out. Keep the soil round it moist and spray the leaves and branches overhead, two or three times a week at least. Do not attempt to plunge the pot this way if the garden soil is limy. In the autumn and before the frosts take up the plant, scrub the pot clean and bring indoors again. But please do not expect the same magnificence of bloom that there was on the plant when it first came to you.

So far as size is concerned, all tastes are catered for. The small pots of azaleas are most endearing I think. They are as flower-studded considering their size as any of the giants. They are, too, most tenacious so long as they are cared for.

Here perhaps I should explain a little more about these plants, like azaleas, which prefer an acid soil. Indeed "prefer" is too mild a term for most of them cannot live in any soil that contains lime. This acid soil consists mainly of peat. Although the lime-haters are in the minority so far as pot-plants are concerned the few include some of the most familiar, azaleas, heaths (ericas) and rhododendrons.

It is this passion for acidity which makes them such difficult plants to keep alive year after year unless you live on acid soil. A further point is the character of root growth. Soon the pot becomes filled with roots so fibrous that it becomes most difficult to see which is compost and which is peat. Peat is very porous but once it becomes dry it shrinks. If the root ball is allowed to get dry it shrinks and pulls away from the sides of the pot. It is possible to soak the plant and so re-charge it— I once saw a plant that had been allowed to become so dry that the root ball left the pot in the bottom of the bucket and sailed up to the water level.

Once this drying out takes place, even if the pot is re-soaked it will never be the same again. In the first place water is never so efficient because of that narrow gap between root ball and pot. The water courses down that and escapes. After drying out in this way the plant ought always to be soaked for watering

Unfortunately these peat loving plants are brought into our homes mainly at the Christmas season. At this time our homes get too hot and too dry and we get forgetful. Unless we give the plant a drink immediately we receive it the poor thing can dry out and so be given its knock-out punch overnight.

With the smaller pots, naturally, the process is quicker. The tiny "thumb" pots of heather are already at a disadvantage. These arrive in market not in the pots they have always been grown in but having been knocked out, root trimmed and re-potted in a *smaller* size. They are given a recuperative period at the nursery after this treatment but a check is given. So long as they are never allowed to dry out they do not suffer and should last well. These little plants are ideal for incorporating in mixed arrangements designed as Christmas gifts. Being plunged they are not so likely to suffer from over-dryness.

Cyclamen are good value for money but one should remember that they just cannot live in an atmosphere that becomes polluted with domestic gas—a gas fire, even if it is lit only for a short period each day, will soon cause the leaves to turn yellow and the young buds to die.

These plants can be bought in 60s and in varying sizes (and shapes if you live in the north) of pots up to the 32. As I suggested elsewhere I believe it is a better buy always to get a large potted plant rather than a small one, although I appreciate that this is not always practical.

It doesn't benefit a small flowering cyclamen to re-pot it right away. If you wish to save the plant for another year, re-pot it next season when growth begins.

Cyclamen, or rather their indoor culture, seem to arouse more controversy than any other plant except the African violet. After once writing of them in a national newspaper I was amazed—and gratified—by the number of people who wrote to tell me of their pet theories on the bringing up of a cyclamen. One reader had kept a plant for four years!

One needs to take great care over the watering of cyclamen. The plant grows from a corm, a round brown "root" which sits on the soil. This is done because a buried corm is liable to rot. The cause of the rotting is damp. So the corm is buried only partly in the soil, just enough to anchor it. Another way a corm becomes rotten is when water settles among the stems which spring up from it. For this reason one advises that the plant should not be watered from above but that the water should be poured into the saucer or container and that the pot should take it up that way.

As an example I often quote the method of cultivation in use on a cyclamen nursery I visited in Holland. Here thousands of wonderful plants are grown for seed. Each pot stands in its own saucer. As the nurseryman goes from plant to plant he pours a little water in the saucer. This remains damp all the time. There is a warm, humid atmosphere. This puddle must be a small one though, for the soil in the pot must not remain sodden as it would do if the water was too deep. If you are uncertain it is as well to stand the pot on a little stand made of wood. Two pieces of wood running parallel under the pot will raise it above the puddle. The wood will take up the water and pass it on to the pot. Small pots can be stood on match sticks. Tie two together each side.

Even if the plant is small it can be a good specimen of its kind. There should be a good thick cluster of leaves. There may be only two or three flowers in bloom but there should be a promise of succession by plenty of buds. Individually these little plants are quite charming, but do remember that massed they can look most attractive, especially if the hues are varied.

One advantage that the cyclamen has over other plants is its handsome foliage. Not only are the leaves prettily shaped but many of them are beautifully marked or marbled. All the undersides are contrasting with a reddish hue but some are quite vivid. However should extra foliage be needed to complete an arrangement the ornamental *Begonias rex* look well with cyclamen and as similar conditions suit them the plants should thrive.

The cyclamen has a long season. The first plants begin to

43

come on to the market at the end of September and finish some time in March. Unless you are a good gardener do not expect your own plant to flower continuously over this period.

The primulas I mentioned earlier differ from each other quite considerably. Of them I should say that *Primula obconica* is the best buy. This is the primula which is reputed to give an allergy to some people—but one should say in all fairness that many plants do this and fortunately their victims are few and scattered. The trouble is that until you handle the plant you will not know if you are allergic to it, but please believe me that it is nothing like so venomous as legend would give us to believe.

At one time this primula, like so many of our temporary plants, flowered in winter or early spring, but nowadays they can be bought in flower all year round. The reason for this and indeed for the all-the-year-round supply of flowering pot plants, is the greater appreciation of their value for window-boxes and foyer groups and other decoration of this kind.

Primula obconica is not only perennial, it might almost be called perpetual flowering. One should take care to remove faded flowers and when all have bloomed to cut away down to an inch or so from the base the stem on which now only the green calyces are left. Keep the plant supplied with food especially while it carries blooms and never let it become dry. Use the paddling method for watering and let the pot stand in at least a quarter inch of water. If the plants stand on a sunny window-sill, keep a careful eye on them, for evaporation can be very rapid. See that no moisture is splashed on the leaves when they are in this position or they may become spotted brown.

So many people are making a hobby of growing saintpaulias or African violets and nothing else, that I can recommend you (should you also be a slave to their charms) to join one or other of the African violet societies who will help you tremendously.

I have been in trouble before and shall be again for saying that I do not consider these an easy indoor plant. I think they are absolutely charming but because we have the smallest amount of gas in our atmosphere in London they will not thrive. But with some people they appear to tumble over themselves to bloom.

Once established they are almost ever-blooming so long as the faded flowers are removed and not allowed to seed. The plants produce masses of flowers—new ones are almost two inches across—which much resemble violets. This similarity is more marked in varieties which have violet coloured blooms. Others are white, pink, rose, lavender and blue. Actually they vary considerably in foliage as well as bloom.

They will grow happily in a window on the shady side of the house for they do not demand brilliant sunshine—a great point in their favour. But one should not expect many winter flowers from a plant in such an aspect. Saintpaulias prefer east and west windows. Grown in a south facing window they should not be set too near the glass for there is danger from the sun burning the leaves.

Hairy or downy leaved plants are often susceptible to sun-burning. If droplets of moisture adhere to the hairs they act as a magnifying glass would do if sunlight were allowed to pass through it while it was focused on the leaf surface. This danger can be avoided if the plants are watered as they should be, from the base, or from water entering the pores of the pot through some medium such as damp peat into which the plant is plunged. Their roots should be kept moist all the time.

Specialists recommend that the soil should not be made too firm, a point to bear in mind when re-potted. Plants are best re-potted annually. They may also be divided. Best of all, they root easily if leaf cuttings are taken in water or moist sand.

Many of the hydrangeas we see growing near the front door of a suburban house or cottage began life as a pot plant. There are several species of hydrangea but the one grown as a pot plant is hortensia. This has many varieties. I can remember when the only colours available were pink, white, and the unbelievable blue so typical of this flower. Now the varieties bring a wealth of colour.

There is a difference too in the nature of the plant itself. The mop heads or mops, one great flower cluster on one stem which constituted the entire plant, were once greatly sought after. Those were the days when banks of flowering plants were built up as indoor decorations. Now, when more people want to have just one good plant, the fashion is to grow a plant with more stems and smaller clusters.

The hydrangea is a good buy for if you choose a young plant and look after it well it should last for many weeks. Botanically it differs from the usual pot flowers. The pretty petals are really bracts, a leafy collar which surrounds a tiny flower which when in young bud may be as small as a pin's head. In the very young stage these bracts are green then they gradually take on their floral hue. After the real flowers, the tiny ones, have bloomed and faded the coloured bracts persist. Out of doors where the plant grows naturally these remain on the bushes often turning the most delightful variety of hues and sometimes persisting, green again now, right through the winter.

Indoors the "flowers" do not mature in quite the same way. In fact if the plant has been grown "soft" the bracts just flop and fade after the flower is finished, but not always, instead the plant goes on in "bloom" for many weeks.

When choosing a hydrangea plant examine the bloom heads for these tiny flowers. The more there are that are unopened the better. The tiny buds look a little like coloured hot-cross buns! If one or more of the bloom heads are still green or only just turning colour so much the better for this way you are bound to have a succession of colour. Cut off any flagged or faded blooms should these occur.

Hydrangeas are greedy plants. The grower feeds and cares for their wants unceasingly as he brings them to perfection.

They come to market and are sold and abruptly all these things
are withheld from them. The strange thing is that so many go on
living, not that some fade. Of course much of the plant food is
still there in the pot and the water makes it available to the
plant in solution. But I think it is a good thing to feed the
hydrangea from the time it comes to you. Use plant tablets, a
pinch of powdered plant food, dried blood or liquid manure,
given according to the directions for flowering plants. This way
too one builds up the plant's vitality so that it will throw out
good leaf growths after flowering.

The pot of a hydrangea plant is usually very full of roots and
often they can be seen like a network on the surface. For this
reason it is best to immerse the pot, so that the rim is just
covered, in a bowl or bucket of water. Allow it to remain in the
water until no more bubbles rise from the soil. You will need
to do this every day in hot weather.

Although it is not intended to deal with bulb flowers as such
in this book one cannot really discuss indoor plants without
referring to them. For many people, growing a hyacinth bulb
in a glass of water is the extent of their indoor gardening acti-
vities. To others, fortunately, it is the beginning.

Many people, whether they grow indoor plants or not, have
for years grown a few bulbs indoors. Some have been doing it
from childhood, others grow bulbs for Christmas presents. So
this is nothing new and I do not propose to devote much space
to the subject here. It is covered adequately elsewhere.

Bulbs grown indoors have got to be pretty good to stand up
to the artificial way they are grown, so it is unwise to buy
bargain batches. Go for the good, big, fat bulbs from reputable
firms. Remember, that bulbs have the embryo flower already
in them, so they must be treated gently and carefully. "Treated" bulbs have been given an artificial winter, they have been
pre-cooled so that they will flower earlier. Hyacinths are best
for forcing this way indoors and it is quite easy to have some

in flower for Christmas. The narcissus Cragford, if pre-cooled, can also be grown quite easily this way. It bears several flowers on one stem.

Generally speaking, it is wise to plant your indoor bulbs as soon as they are received from your merchant or as soon as you see them available in the shops. This will be from September onwards. Bulb fibre is the usual medium. This is a mixture of peat, charcoal and shell. But clean, washed pebbles or even garden soil will do quite well, as well as plain water for hyacinths. Bulb fibre comes dry in bags and it should be moistened before use, not after. Best put it into a bucket of water and allow it to soak for a little while. But don't use it while it is too wet. Scoop out handfuls and squeeze them so that the water runs away and you are left with a firm ball of the damp moisture. This is the dampness and the moisture content that is best.

Plant so that the nose of the bulb is just above the fibre level and so that bulbs are close to each other but not touching. Don't use too shallow bowls or the growing roots will force the bulbs up above the fibre.

When they have all been planted, keep the bulbs in a cool dark place for a few weeks. They can be out of doors if you like, preferably buried under peat or washed ashes and clinker. If they are indoors, they should be in the dark and they should be inspected periodically to make sure they are not dry. Bulbs must never be allowed to dry out.

In about six or eight weeks a root system will have been formed and the nose may be showing a green shoot. They can now be taken out of their cool spot and brought into the light and a slightly warmer place. But don't transfer them to a really warm and stuffy atmosphere at once.

As the foliage and flowers grow upwards, it is wise to turn the pots daily so that the light reaches them from all sides. Otherwise they will grow towards the light and you will be left with uneven plants. When they have finished flowering, let the foliage die down naturally, just as you do in the garden. Do not cut it away or you will reduce the ability of the bulb to store new energy. The bulbs can be planted in the garden, even after they are forced, but it is possible that they will not produce flowers for a year or two.

Hyacinths, daffodils and tulips are not the only bulb flowers that will grow well indoors. This year we had some really wonderful crocus flowers from bulbs which my husband brought back from a grower in the north of Holland. (Incidentally, and as a matter of interest, this grower had seven sons, all working on the bulb farm. Whew!) Snowdrops, scillas and muscari can also be grown indoors, but of course these do not produce the same quantity of bloom.

The season for planting bulbs is a fairly tight one. You can't leave it too long or you will be too late. Commercial growers know this and those who grow bulbs devote a good bit of their time to arranging their schedules to coincide with the planting season and very soon after bulbs have been planted they are available in the shops and markets all planted up and ready for the living room.

However this chapter is intended to suggest good plants for a beginner and good buys. Buy bulbs such as hyacinths, tulips and daffodils growing in plain flower pots, rather than those in bowls. The former are more likely to have been grown slower and accordingly will last longer. Bulbs that have been very forced mature rapidly. It is likely, though by no means a universal practice, that the attractive "made-up" bowl of bulb flowers has been assembled from bulbs "ex-pot". Should you wish you can assemble attractive arrangements of your own this way.

It is safe to buy any bulb flower in bud. Indeed this is recommended unless the flowers are needed for immediate decoration. Most people enjoy watching the buds coming slowly into bloom.

There is no need to feed the plants but they should never be allowed to dry out. After the flowers have faded cut them off just below the "neck". Do not cut away any leaves even if they turn brown. The leaves of a bulb plant are needed to store up food in the bulb after it has flowered so that it has strength enough to flower another year. In some cases the base of the stem actually swells to form the new bulb.

Water a little less after flowering, and when the leaves have died down withhold water altogether so that they shrivel. When it is possible to lift out, (not pull out), the shrivelled leaves the bulb may be taken out of the soil and re-potted in fresh soil if you wish to try to grow them indoors again. This is not recommended since bulbs once forced do not always flower the following year. Bulbs may be planted in the garden from bowls or pots at any stage. It is not necessary to wait for them to die down.

If you like daisies you must admire the cinerarias, those exotic multi-coloured blooms that originated in the Canaries. The parent species, *Senecio cruenta*, was purple but now thanks to the plant breeder there are white, sugar-pink, fiery magenta, vivid blue, pale blue, midnight blue and violet either self coloured or banded with a contrasting hue. Like the hydrangeas the large mop-head type of plant has lost favour although some are still grown. Instead a smaller flowered, well branching and very much wirier type is favoured.

The daisy like blooms are borne in clusters and like all daisies are long lasting. A good plant will also have budding stems springing from the axils of the leaves. As and when a flower dies cut it away from the rest of the bunch otherwise the plant is liable to concentrate (if plants *can* be said to concentrate) on producing seed from the finished flower rather than to produce more blooms from the existing shoots.

Cinerarias are gross feeders. They need plenty of water and feeding regularly, say every two weeks. Although they are botanically perennials these plants are grown as annuals. It is not worth while trying to save the plant from one year to the next, although if you have a greenhouse it is possible to take cuttings of any variety that takes your fancy.

Cinerarias are winter or summer flowering.

No collection of house plants could possibly be complete without a geranium although I must confess that I have met a few people who said that they could not bear them. Subsequently I discovered that they knew only the vivid scarlet variety. Many people find this a fierce not-easy-to-live-with colour. A large number of those who discovered that they could get a similar variety in pure white, soft pink or magenta completely changed their attitude.

The familiar red geranium, technically a zonal pelargonium, has green leaves with a defined but not striking zone of contrasting colour. However there are other geraniums whose foliage is striking and more colourful than the flowers. The leaves are vivid orange, yellow and green, or green, white and red, all kinds of variations in fact.

It might be well just to have a quick run through some of the geraniums in their various classifications and to do so I have looked out the catalogue of a well-known geranium specialist to provide the very latest information in this fast moving field.

The largest group is contained under the label zonal geranium or pelargonium and of the single varieties all have five petals. The most famous is Paul Crampel, probably the most frequently seen geranium in outdoor bedding schemes. It is probably in every public park in the country.

The doubles and semi-doubles can have any number of petals over five. Gustav Emich is the best known here. This is the famous geranium in the beds in front of Buckingham Palace. Its colour matches exactly the scarlet of the guardsmen's jackets. Incidentally, double geraniums make long lasting cut flowers. They were used many years ago as a popular buttonhole flower and I have heard old-timers speak of the days when they used to sell a geranium flower for twopence and a half geranium (split right down the centre of the stem and flower with a razor blade) for a penny.

Still in the zonal class, there are rosebud, bird's egg, cactus flowered, miniature and fancy-leaved varieties. The names are all descriptive. Of these I will mention only another famous geranium, Mr. Henry Cox, which although technically a tricolour in the fancy leaved group, has foliage of pale gold marked with purple, red, cream and green. The single flowers are rose coloured.

The ivy-leaved geraniums are perhaps not so suitable for growing indoors as others, but I have grown one so successfully and for so many years that I have become particularly attached to this group. My friend is L'Elegante, and I freely admit that its flowers are insignificant compared to its foliage, for the leaves are dark green variegated with cream and have a strong blush of purple in them. I have had one growing in a large glazed vase without any drainage hole for many years. It stands in a window in my bedroom at our country home and it has grown immense in this time.

The scented-leaved geraniums are also favourites of mine. They really are scented, too, and some are used as a perfume base while all are popular in gardens for the blind. Some of the scents identifiable are: rose, lemon, balsam, pine, nutmeg, orange and peppermint. (I cannot forbear to quote that in this group appears a rose-scented variety called Little Gem. It seems that it was once called Terebinthinaceum!)

Then there are the species and I note with nostalgia here that there are said to be between two and three hundred wild species of pelargonium but only a few in commerce. When I was very much younger and had very much more spare time and very much more energy, I often thought how wonderful a field lay here for investigation, experimentation and inter-breeding. Am I really too late?

Geraniums like sun and fairly dry conditions. Do not immerse them to water them. In most cases water once a week should be sufficient. Do not attempt to grow them on the shady or north side of the house for there is not sufficient sun to encourage flowers or good leaf colour.

The sweet smelling *Rochea coccinea*, (sometimes called crassula) is a good buy. The scarlet flowers bloom in summer on foot high stalks covered with thick fleshy leaves. There is also a spring flowering white and pink species called *versicolor*. These plants like the sun and are ideal for a sunny window. When the flowers are over—and they last a long time—the stems should be pruned right down to about an inch or to a young shoot.

I mention them not only because I think you would be pleased to know about them but because they introduce us to a type of plant which differs considerably from the usual. These are the succulents. Not many of them are grown as house plants but they deserve to be better known.

Succulents are just as their name suggests, plants with thick succulent leaves and/or stems. A plant known to millions is the seaside daisy that is encouraged to scramble over cliff sides or promenade gardens binding the soil and giving a continuous succession of vivid flowers.

Succulents are plants which have adapted themselves to stand long periods of drought, like the desert prickly pear cactus. The stone-crop growing on the crown of a stone wall, the house-leek on a cottage roof are both succulents. The fact that they are so full of moisture enables them to live while no water or air moisture is available. Unfortunately, there exists a fallacy that the poor plants need no water. How often one hears someone say: "Oh cactus! They don't need watering do they?" We have to remember that under natural conditions there are occasions when they become well watered—some times even flooded.

Cacti and all other types of succulents do need water. Give them a really good drink once a month. At the same time give them plenty of sun and light. I have found that they will tolerate a much cooler atmosphere than one might at first expect until one remembers that desert nights are cool too as well as sometimes wet!

You cannot go far wrong with any of these succulents. All cacti are not covered with spines looking like prickly pincushions. The prickly pear, the tall column-like varieties and the leaf-flowering cactus are all fascinating. The latter is sometimes known as the Christmas cactus or because of the shape of its flattened leaf-like stems, as the crab cactus. In winter the ends of the stems produce the loveliest rosy red flowers which, probably because of their pendant habit, always remind me of Christmas tree decorations. This particular plant, to prove my point, will actually die if it is not given sufficient to drink.

Although the beauty if a cactus plant is not appreciated by all, some of the other types of succulents have an immediate appeal. They grow rosette-like, each leaf beautifully alternating with the one below it. To me they look like great fleshy flowers. They are extremely handsome. One I have, an *Aeonium tabuliforme*, has a rosy tinge and the leaves are covered with a soft grey bloom.

Now these are obviously plants for the indoor gardener who has not yet mastered the intricacies of careful watering. With any of these installed you can say to yourself "These will I water on the first of every month!"

Certainly this might be a good rule to follow if one is uncertain or ignorant, but after growing cacti for some time one soon becomes aware of the needs of the plants. In the summer months, for example, considerably more water can be absorbed by the plants and in the winter if the cacti are kept in a fairly warm room, they will again require watering at more frequent intervals.

I had one startling experience of a cactus plant, one of the mamillarias, which I kept for some years in the country. It was planted again in a glazed Italian pot, without drainage hole and for this reason as well as its natural disinclination for too much moisture I suppose I gave it water about once a month on the average. It lived for some years, making little or no progress but appearing quite healthy. Then a year or two ago during a hot spell I tried doubling the watering rate. The plant responded at once by putting on weight and size. I was tempted to even give more, but I stayed my hand and for a few summer weeks merely gave double the normal rate and that little mammillaria grew and grew, still with the same, fine, healthy look about it.

I would like to say that it flourishes still. But alas! it had to be left for a considerable period in a very cold spell last winter and when we were next in the country it was looking very unhappy. The lower part had blackened, obviously frosted, and there was a distinct list to starboard. Out of pure interest I refrained from touching it and noticed that the blackening spread up the plant to the crown. Eventually it keeled right over and dropped, soft and limp, over the edge of the pot. The centre had previously become hollow and at its last gasp the plant exuded the last final drops of moisture it contained, and these, black, concentrated and sticky, oozed down the side of the container.

I was sorry to see it go, for it had been an old friend, but I felt that I had learned something from its passing and I was grateful.

In the summer months air is important and cactus plants should either be placed outside in the sun or can go on the windowsill *outside* the window. But keep an eye on them. Don't let them be caught in a downpour more than once in a while and don't let them be knocked over by windy gusts. If they must stay indoors, in a city, for example, open the windows and let them get some fresh air.

I may be wrong, but I imagine that cacti are largely a male taste. I think we women go rather more for colour and beauty of form rather than sheer curiosity and grotesquerie. Certainly, my husband's collection, which sits in front of the window beside his desk, is growing—and flourishing. Even I will occasionally bring him home in triumph a new and particularly ugly specimen that I have seen somewhere.

Because these plants face due south and get a good deal of sun, they are watered comparatively frequently. But instead of using conventional methods, the pots are taken out of their outer containers and the plant and pot are given a thorough but gentle spraying with clean water. They appear to respond to this treatment and a number of baby plants in the form of plantlets, offsets and tubercles are appearing, some of which are in the process of being rooted.

Although it is not necessary that the baby plants, offsets, opuntia pads or tubercles should be removed, they can be snapped off quite easily and will quickly take root if planted in John Innes seed compost in late April or May when the weather is getting warm. It is sometimes productive of a more curiously shaped plant to leave the odd babies still in position, but removing them not only increases your stock but also gives the parent plant a better chance of growing.

Many of these plants will root well if portions are removed with a very sharp knife or razor blade and planted in the usual fashion. At some nurseries, particularly a very famous one in Holland, cuttings are rooted in pure, dry peat and although from personal observation I can testify that the most successful results are obtained, I have never tried this myself, although I shall obviously have to do so if only to satisfy my curiosity.

Another activity concerned with cacti that I have not yet

tried is grafting. It is possible to take cuttings from many plants and to insert them in V-shaped cuts in another plant, holding them in position with string, a sharpened matchstick or a cactus spine until the graft has taken. In this way even more grotesque shapes and forms may be obtained.

It seems to me (and I must admit that this is a subject about which I know little, though I am learning) that to get really strange, really large and really splendid cacti specimens it is necessary to grow them yourself. Although there are several cacti specialists in this country the vast majority of specimens which they sell are ordinary, run of the mill varieties, fairly small in size. It is possible to obtain outsize plants and it is possible to buy unusual plants, but not with the same facility with which one can obtain the unusual house plant or the unusual outdoor shrub or tree. My own belief is that this is such an absorbing interest that even the commercial grower jealously guards his own prize specimens and will not let them go. At the nursery in Holland, for example, nearly all of one huge glasshouse is taken up with the proprietor's own plants. He will permit, even invite, customers to look at these and admire them, but he has apparently refused to consider the most fantastic offers to buy them. I rather like that attitude.

Some plants have the same 'love for drought conditions but their leaves are tough and leathery rather than succulent. Of these one that I recommend is the sansevieria or unkindly mother-in-law's tongue (because it is long, sharp and pointed). This is an extremely handsome plant. It comes from tropical West Africa and looks it! The pale green leaves are banded with dark green and bordered, all the way round, with yellow.

One fault we have found with sansevieria in small pots is that unless they are set inside another, heavier and bulkier container there is danger of them tipping over and so becoming damaged. One needs to watch this point. We have overcome it, and gained a more attractive decoration into the bargain by choosing urns and the modern tripod tube container to hold their pots. This way they look most elegant. Other tough leaved plants—all incidentally good sunny window plants—are the agave, or aloe of which many species are in cultivation, most of them originating from Mexico.

Generally speaking then, the succulents and the leathery leaved plants are good subjects for a beginner. You do not have to confine your decorations to rows of little pots on window-box or window-table, and anyway this style of gardening calls for too intricate dusting. Here is also the danger of knocking over little pots. Cacti and succulents can be plunged or planted either in bowls or more ambitious community centres.

What about those permanent plants which because of the publicity which has been given them in all kinds of newspapers and magazines have come to be known as the house plants? These are the erect, thick leaved ficus, the trailers, the climbers, the sprawlers and the crawlers. Where do we begin with these?

Without hesitation I award the palm (no pun intended) to the hedera, the ivy, for it has several forms, all easy, all decorative, all tolerant and all flexible. Many people confuse the popular *Hedera helix Chicago* (paradoxically the "English" ivy of the Americans) with the common wild ivy which grows everywhere in this island, on trees, walls and in hedgerows. Obviously they are relatives but Chicago is a variety not one of our native species. It is a carefully cultivated plant with a dainty softer habit, a more attractive and leafier growth, a much branching, finer and more flexible stem. Neither, unfortunately, is it as tough and hardy as its wild relative. However, you can induce the wild ivy to grow indoors. To mask its legginess it is best to make a corkscrew type of support so that the trails can be taken round and round spirally.

New varieties and species of hedera are appearing on the market constantly. One of the prettiest of recent introductions is *Hedera glacier*, small, tough-leaved, ice-white edged with a grey surface over the main fabric of the leaves. It will take happily to cooler conditions and produces a profusion of dainty foliage that will climb and trail as desired. It looks very attractive arranged with some of the darker, glossier leaved types.

There are other variegated ivies. These are tabled at the end of the book. All are, in my opinion, worth growing but not all are as tough as glacier which incidentally in spite of its name will not stand frost.

For a long time the only variegated ivy available as a pot plant was *Hedera canariensis*. But we have always found this a little more temperamental than most ivies. It dislikes too frequent watering and yet cannot survive drought. On being established in a room it quite often makes its début by shedding its leaves. Should this happen pinch out the growing point or points if the plant has several stems to induce it quickly to put out fresh leaves. Try to adjust the watering. Let the soil dry out before giving more water and do not allow it to paddle.

If you can grow this plant, and many people do bringing it to a perfection of size and colour, you will have one of the handsomest of the ivies. This ivy is said to have originated in the Canary Islands. Its leaves look as if each has passed through the hands of a water colour artist. Primrose yellow, light and dark and grey green are attractively blotched one on the other.

For indoor gardeners looking for a large leaved indoor plant the Ravenholst ivy is magnificent. I have two plants one of which has grown steadily up from the mantelshelf (there is no fire ever beneath, the room is heated another way) until it found the warm air current and then began to cascade prettily out towards the window, four feet away, and downwards to trail over the mantel edge. The leaves vary from three inches across to an inch and a half of the young foliage. They have such a natural sheen that I am always being asked how I treat them to make them shine.

The other is nine feet high a tall slender pillar of green flanking the french-door to my roof garden in London. Seen against the lettuce green of the woodwork it looks most effective. This variety likes light but not too much sun and appears not to like too much water. Ours are always slightly dry being watered no oftener than once a week and although we haven't central heating we like our rooms warm.

Probably because I have a liking for the more clinging type of plant I prefer Ravenholst to the dominant *Ficus decora* or so called rubber plant, although I must admit there is none other quite like this particular fig, for "fig" it is! Its large shiny leaves looking like good green leather are most handsome. And it seems adaptable. I was shown one recently which shared a bowl garden with an assortment of other plants and was doing extremely well, growing slowly but really growing not standing dormant. This little garden belonged to a friend who watered it "every Monday". The room in which they grew was not so light but they lived at the side of the window and flourished there. Another friend has a young giant which grows in the corner of her room between the window and the door.

Anthony Huxley in his little but most comprehensive book on house plants suggests that in some towns the tap water is detrimental to the ficus but we have not found it so, however it is a point to bear in mind. Anyway, it is always better to use rain water for all plants if it can be collected.

It seems to me that *Ficus decora* is one of those plants that will grow anywhere for in one of Odhams' photographic studios there is a plant of it growing full pelt ahead in the glaring sun with never a leaf lost or spotted. Yet one is often recommended not to stand this plant in direct sunshine. This particular ficus is subjected to extremes of normal light and studio lighting which is very fierce. Yet it and some others in the same studio are flourishing and thrive under treatment which to me is quite alarming! In fact so well are they doing that one date palm has not only put forth new leaves but also two branches of flowers! Something very rare indeed.

Among the ficus family are many excellent house plants with more being introduced all the time. (The original demand for house plants has now changed to a demand for "new" house plants. This has stimulated trade and exchange between many countries and I find it most exciting to be asked, every so often, to come along and see the newcomers.) This fig family is really most diverse. Some species seem at first meeting to have no relating features, leaves are varied in texture and shape, stems are tree-like or creeping or climbing. We have to remember that botanists group plants according to relating features of their flowers. With plants such as we are discussing we seldom if ever see their flowers—even if we did we might not even then easily recognize relationships.

However it is this diversity that adds to their interest. With the ficus family it is safe to say that all that are sold as such are good house plants. If we find a good family, one that we can get along with, it is as well to cultivate it in more ways than one. There is a splendid example of the practicability of the technical term. Given only folk names we would need to be specialists to recognize relationships in plants. As it is all we need to do is to glance at the label. The Latin name tells us all we need to know.

One of the easiest of the figs is the little *Ficus pumila* I mentioned earlier. This needs a lot of water most of the time. The leaves are small and round and the stems will trail most attractively over the edge of a container while taller stems can be induced to climb if they are assisted. The fiddle-leaf fig *Ficus lyrata* is similar in habit to the *Ficus decora* except that the leaves are not so symmetrical. They are in fact fiddle-shaped.

If you have a passion for variegated plants there is a variegated form of *Ficus decora*. A trailer similar in habit and in its

needs is the green and white *Ficus radicans*. If allowed to dry
out there is no chance of saving this plant. So grow it where it
can be sprayed or easily removed for spraying. If you have a
garden room you can encourage it to climb the wall, which like
its cousin pumila it will do most attractively.

It is only natural that once one member of a plant family gets
a reputation for being a good doer that growers should seek
out other relatives. This has happened with the ficus tribe.
There are now several species. So far none I have seen could
possibly be confused with the other. All are individualists. There
is one particular point in their favour which might further
endear them to you. They will grow in a non-sunny aspect,
windows on the north and east of the house will suit them well
if you are looking for tenants for these positions. If you should
grow them there remember that growth is sure to be slower
with less light. This means that water and food should not be
given too liberally.

Making its début about the same time as the contemporary
ficus was the heart-shaped leaved *Philodendron scandens*. We
have had several of these attractive climbers and for a year now
have been growing a plant in our bathroom. I was prompted to
do so by the comment of an American visitor who on seeing a
philodendron in our living room claimed that "there was one
in every bathroom in the States!" In fact he calls it the bathroom plant.

Our room has a gas heater. A flue for fumes is attached and
although I have never smelt gas there one assumes that the air
must be polluted if only to a small degree. The only daylight
filters through a small fan-light in the ceiling. This can be
opened for ventilation, but it never is. In spite of all this, the
philodendron was placed on a shelf, its 60 pot sunk in Florapak inside a white urn. It has to exist on little daylight and the
electric light which is switched on whenever anyone uses the
room. It has not died but on the other hand it has not increased.

There it stands as it was on the day we acquired it, filling up a bare corner and looking green and fresh. As they say in book reviews "warmly recommended".

Some *Philodendron scandens* are sold supported by cork bark into which they may also anchor their aerial roots. This way they are grown as upright plants but you may also use this plant as a climber or trailer. Unless it is kept well fed and given plenty of light an active plant can become leggy. The internodes lengthen especially during winter. The best remedy for this is in March to cut right back to a good leaf—details are given in a later chapter.

There are now many other species of philodendron and they look like producing some of the most exciting and handsome of our house plants. *Philodendron erubescens* is one of the loveliest plants. The leaves are very large, shiny and most decorative. The philodendron—its name by the way denotes that it is wet loving and tree-growing—belongs to a group of plants called Aroids which are all in the Arum family. As a point of interest our native aroid is the Cuckoo-pint or Lords and Ladies which flowers in the hedgerows in spring. Take a good look at its leaves if you get a chance and you will see a pattern for a great variation of vegetative themes.

One plant I have, which I recommend as an easy to grow species if you can give it good but not glaring light, is *Syngonium velozianum*. It has grown three feet this year and is now over five feet. At an early stage in its life it was started off against a cork bark support but that has long since been left behind and is now assisted by plastic transparent stakes. On it goes, up and up like Jack's beanstalk, but from its stems grow out tough little arrow shaped leaves almost identical with those that grow in the damp air of the ditch which drains my country garden. These are the little grey hens! Other aroids are remarkable for their brilliance, the caladiums, dieffenbachias.

There are many people who do not want plants trailing,

climbing and creeping about their walls and furniture but who want an attractive plant that will furnish and decorate their rooms. Many such plants can be found among the aroids. If you grow them well you may be rewarded with flowers, odd, exotic, green arum lily like structures, the collectors' items of the horticultural world.

Among the handsome foliage plants are the *Begonia rex*, the ornamental leaved begonias. Here is another good buy. The plants will provide an all the year round feast of glorious and subtle colour combinations. Characteristic of this species of begonia is the metallic sheen which covers and shines from the upper surface of the leaf. Silver, grey, purple, rose, red are all mingled most beautifully.

Most of the leaves are spade-shaped with one side larger than the other but one variety called *stellata* is, as its name suggests, star shaped.

A friend of mine has a magnificent plant growing on the flat base of the stair banister in her hall. This hall is walled on the door side with reeded glass and it seems that sufficient light reaches the plant for in the year it has been there it has grown so well. It is now a mass of stars, each borne on long stems which themselves fall gracefully making a most attractive decoration.

One is usually recommended to keep these begonias on the damp side but I must confess that when I discovered that my plant in the country was doing quite well in a south facing window with a drink once a week or less frequently I have been allowing the town plants to dry out more too. They are all thriving. At a lecture I gave in Taunton someone pointed out that the pictures showed the begonia leaves to have long stems. This lady was keen on floral arrangement and liked to pick the rex leaves but found them difficult to use because of their short stems. After some discussion we decided that mine had probably grown longer because of the drier conditions.

Plants can be made to catch the eye or divert attention, in this case from the empty fireplace. Beneath the large-leaved *Hedera ravenholst* grows *H. glacier*. On the right is the little umbrella plant *Cyperus diffusus* which needs to paddle in water. A cyclamen is in the centre.

A mirror makes a narrow room appear wider and also reflects a great deal of light, which is helpful to plants. Growing well back in the room and reflected in the mirror is *Monstera deliciosa*. To the left before the mirror are *H. ravenholst*, *Begonia rex*, and on the right near a french window, is *Cobea scandens*. The begonia must not remain back in a room although it does not like direct sun-glare through glass. Its position should be changed from time to time.

Incidentally the star-leaved variety is also watered only once weekly.

Probably the most striking of all our house plants is the *Monstera deliciosa*, sometimes called the Gruyère cheese plant because of the characteristic holes in its leaves. There appears to be only one of its kind in cultivation at the present time. It is not a plant for the small home for its leaves are really large. As a rule it doesn't make rapid growth. One sees it more often as a specimen plant standing against a wall rather than climbing up it. Recently my husband was across the Channel and visited a quayside *bistro*. To his amazement there he saw a monstera which had not only climbed up the wall for several feet but also along the top of the window too. He took a picture of it for me to see. Just a few weeks before we had seen another monstera which had thrilled us. A friend of ours, the clever carnation and all-the-year-round chrysanthemum grower Graham Sparkes, grows house plants as a hobby but not at home! He has a large garage-like structure with plenty of windows and whitewashed walls. In this building is a fascinating collection of plants in tubs, boxes and pots. In one of the tubs a really fine monstera was growing in flower and in fruit.

It is the quality of the fruit which gives the monstera its specific name deliciosa. We bought some fruits one Christmas. They are long and a little like an unopened cone. When ready to eat the cone disintegrates into small honeycomb shaped sections which taste like a mixture of pineapple and banana. That same Christmas I bought some avocado pears. One I took on television to show how to plant the stone. It was set on top of a glass mustard jar of water. Unusually the root had already begun to shoot which was a great advantage. The plant is now before me a foot high, well endowed with leaves and shoots and still growing in water but anchored by pebbles.

Another great favourite which does not appear on many house plant lists is the plectranthus. My plant was given me three years ago by a friend and all the other little plectranthus dotted about in my two homes (some in soil and some in water) have been pinched off the parent plant. One on the wall above my head as I write, a cutting growing in a green glass wall vase, filling the water with white cotton-like roots, was taken on a television programme and has never stopped growing since.

The parent plant lived for three years on the sill of a very sunny window in the cottage where it used to smother the sill and get very dry, (for it is only in a 60 pot), during the intervals we were away. Because of this its leaves turned a lovely wine red underneath while the stem internodes, the spaces on the stem between the leaves, were bright red. We brought it to town with many other plants this winter and much of the colouring has lightened because it gets less light and is looked after a little too well. I shall take one of its rooted cuttings back to the country when we return.

I should point out that it is now growing in a completely different aspect and position. The following will demonstrate just how much certain plants will tolerate. The plant will have been in my hands four years this spring. It is in its original pot. Not only has it been brought from a very sunny window and the clear air of the country but it is now set back at least six feet from a town window. In this position it gets less light, naturally. Instead of sprawling on the warm window sill the plant now is in a black metal container and its stems, quite heavy incidentally, are supported by strands of white cotton. It measures 41 inches across from tip of curving stem to tip. Another 32 inch trail hangs right down over the pot and eight shoots grow upward.

The contrast of town and country growth is very marked. From the heart of the plant we have the thick red stems and the vividly marked leaves I described earlier, then almost suddenly the plant breaks into a finer, lighter green growth. All these new stems are growing upwards, some at right angles to the old stem.

Incidentally this plant seldom loses its leaves. Mine in spite of its age and ill-treatment has leaves down to soil level. The new leaves are much smaller and the internodes longer. But the plant is alive and obviously flourishing.

Just below it on a shelf I have a bowl pebble garden in which all kinds of cuttings are growing. After hanging the plectranthus I noticed a stem had snapped and was flagging slightly. I cut it away from the plant, cut off its tip and pushed this in the pebble garden, to take root and to take its chance with the rest. Finding that I was left with a stem several inches long, I divided it to see if this too would root. I divided it into three lengths, breaking each piece immediately above a pair of leaves, the lower end of the stem was then set in among the pebbles. These unorthodox cuttings rooted well and have now "broken", their new shoots growing faster every day.

Another plant left very much to its own devices until we brought it to town was variegated *Fatshedera lizei*. This plant and its green form, is one I would heartily recommend to everyone looking for an amiable house plant. Its leaves much resemble the lobed foliage of ivy and it is natural that they should do so for fatshedera is the offspring of a marriage arranged between the giant leaved bush fatsia and a hedera—hence the name.

You probably know the fatsia quite well. Formerly it was known as aralia now its correct name is dizygotheca. Some people incorrectly call it the castor oil plant. Actually the true castor oil plant, ricinus, makes a lovely pot plant. Its leaves are burnished and bronze-like. It is not hardy. It is sometimes grown in parks in summer bedding schemes but it does not survive the frost. The seed needs to be sown indoors in March.

The fatsia makes a good pot plant, though its growth is fairly rapid and soon needs re-potting. When the pot becomes too big to be practicable the plant can be re-planted in the garden. Or if you have no garden it will grow in a tub on a balcony or outside the door.

To return to our fatshedera: the lizei was growing originally in a 60 pot but has since been moved on to a 48. This grew in the sunny window and like the plectranthus has taken kindly to the move to town.

The one fault with fatshedera is that as the stem grows in height it sheds its leaves and so forms a tall whip-like trunk. It is not always necessary to support this unless the plant shows that it cannot stand on its own. The thing to do is to plant either one or more small fatshedera, in which case you will need to move all to a larger pot or, alternatively choose some other climbing or trailing plant that can be trained up the fatshedera stem.

I have used two plectranthus for this purpose. One is being trained up the stem and the other allowed to cascade over the edge of the pot. As the cuttings were unrooted I did not re-pot this plant, this I shall do later. The cuttings were picked from the main plant and each pushed down a hole made by a pencil. They were then firmed and judging by the present rate of growth, rooted in a week or two.

No one could write about trailers or easy-to-grow plants without extolling the virtues of the tradescantias and zebrinas. If you are an outdoor gardener and have the grass-like, purple flowered *Tradescantia virginiana* in a border you will be struck by the dissimilarity between this and the neat attractively leaved pot plant. The similarity rests between the flowers. Sometimes the indoor plants bloom, but not often.

There are now several tradescantias to be bought but the golden and silver are the most popular, and the easiest of all to grow. The "golden" is yellow and green. The "silver" white and green. Sometimes the leaves are banded with colour and the other half contrasting. All kinds become tinged, or completely coloured with amethyst. All variegation disappears if the plant is given too much water and food and insufficient light.

In order to keep plants that are attractively coloured one

should keep going a constant supply of cuttings. These are very easy to take and details are given in a later chapter.

You can keep the same plant going for several years but it is inclined to get ragged and shabby in appearance. However if you wish to get a really good specimen, re-pot a small pot when it is ready into a 48 or some other container you may have for the purpose. The plant does very well if it is suspended either in a hanging basket or after that fashion. Keep it regularly turned so that all sides get the light and growth is even. Every now and then pinch out a shoot, make a little hole in the surface of the soil of the same pot and push the cutting in. This way you can get a really bushy and handsome plant. Some of the trails will grow very long.

Sometimes the stems turn brown and slightly jelly-like before shrivelling. The stem and leaves below and above the shrivelled portion seem perfectly healthy. The thing to do if this happens is to pinch out the shoot going below the shrivelled portion to directly above the first good leaf. Pinch out the good tip of the portion you have taken from the plant and push it back in the soil.

A near relative of the tradescantias, looking like a larger violet hued edition of them is *Zebrina pendula*.

A plant that has not been on any previous list of mine but which is now established as a firm favourite is the unusual little cyperus. This must not be confused with the garden cyprus, which one friend of mine did because the names are so similar. The cyperus is sometimes called the umbrella plant, for it produces a succession of little green umbrellas of grass ribs in the centre of which are its grass-like flowers. The cyperus is a swamp plant by nature, in fact it is cousin to the papyrus or paper plant, therefore it is just the plant for the heavy handed or generous natured, whichever way you look at it, for it needs to stand in a little water all the time and the soil should be kept moist. It will grow in the little 60 pot for a long time but once the tips of the grasses appear browned then give it a larger pot so that it can get more food. This plant will grow anywhere. One of the finest specimens I see is in the window of a car salesroom in Cirencester which seems most of the time to be in full sun, yet we have a very healthy little plant in a fairly shady corner. The little umbels last a long time. Then when the "grass" is mature the tips of the "ribs" start to brown. When these become too untidy cut the umbel stem off at soil level. This will induce more umbels to develop and give the plant a much tidier appearance.

Obviously Old Glory must not be left out of this beginner's list for this was the plant that started us off along the jungle trail. It is an extremely pretty trailer. Each leaf is compound being tripartite. The leaves are green and silky. The young shoots are bronze and covered with silky hairs. Plants are usually sold with a support. You can induce *Rhoicissus rhomboidea* to trail and climb. A combination of both, as I have suggested earlier, is quite delightful.

At the beginning, when I first acquired the plant and its pot was full of soil, I watered it once a week and less than that during cloudy or wet seasons. Now that so many years have passed and I know the pot must be full of roots I give it water roughly every three days.

This plant will look most unhappy if its roots are sodden. Allow a fine white crust to appear on the top soil before giving more water if you feel unable to judge whether moisture is needed or not. But when you do give it water fill the area between soil and pot rim and allow all of this to be absorbed.

Nearly related yet not at all similar in appearance is the kangaroo vine or *Cissus antarctica*. This plant is best used supported or as a climber. We have an outsize specimen trained round an arch which divides our living room from our kitchen. The leaves are about the size of those of a lime tree, shiny and tooth-edged. They are tough as they should be on a plant which bears such a name. *Cissus antarctica* is tenacious. We have seen more than one example of its determination to live despite the treatment it may receive. It particularly dislikes scorching sun and by the same token, the heat generated by photographers' lamps. One plant we had to photograph reacted by turning its leaves brittle and brown. These fell off and the plant looked naked and unhappy. It was summer, and the air being warm, I stood it outside in every shower for a week or two and stood it meanwhile in a dark corner of the room with the window some six or seven feet away.

Soon new leaves appeared, new leaves that right from the beginning were able to adjust themselves to their new environment. The plant now thrives. So if you need a plant for a fairly shady spot this is it, but do not let it be in any danger from a too bright and hot reading lamp or even from a hot, dry draught of air.

When I first met spathiphyllum I should never have believed that the time would come when I would recommend it as an easy plant. It is an aroid and my first plant, a gift, bore a lovely white arum-lily like flower which bloomed a long, long time. Contrasting with it were the long pointed leaves, dark green and shiny. Now my gardening books tell me that this is a stove plant and that it needs a humid atmosphere and a constant temperature of between 65 and 85 deg. F. but I have found that it has the dogged determination to live usually associated only with the aspidistra. My plant is now three years old. It is in its original pot and this winter has actually thrown up another flower. Here is proof of adaptability if ever there was. When the bloom is over I intend re-potting this spathiphyllum and give it a better chance. I wonder what will happen then?

Incidentally it has been fed regularly and lives near my bed, right on the other side of the room from the window, another witness to my theory that really dark-leaved plants can be stood well away from the light. I have the pot standing in an elegant white urn which has been much photographed in my flower arrangement pictures. The result is most pleasing, a ready made arrangement in dark green and white.

Except for the "annual" climbers already mentioned I know of no other indoor plant that will climb or trail and bloom, but there are others like the spathiphyllum, compact and evergreen which will reward you once a year or so with an exotic flower. The easiest or most adaptable of these is the clivia or amanta-phyllum. The leaves are dark green, thick and strap-like (they need to be kept sponged and dusted) and the flowers lily-like. They come in all hues from soft apricot to deep orange. They are borne on a thick stem, many flowers to the bloom head.

How pleased I am to see that ferns are returning to favour, for these are the most co-operative of house plants richly rewarding their owners for regular watering and a place out of the sun which is really all they demand.

The adiantum, or maidenhair fern, is lovely and brings immediately the impression of dewy grottoes but do not attempt to grow it if your rooms are dry and centrally heated. If by chance it should become over dry the fronds will shrivel and become beyond salvation.

Go instead for the tougher leaved fern, *Nephrolepis cordifolia*. If you find this grows with you and it should share your home for years—get its daintier cousin the lacy ladder fern, *N. exaltata*. I have the two kinds grouped together in one container in my hall-cum-dining room in London where it is always necessary to use artificial light if one reads at table. The ferns flourish.

The pteris or ribbon ferns are hardy too. Keep ferns paddling!

CHAPTER FOUR

PLANTS AS HOME DECORATION

NOTHING can truthfully serve as home decoration if it does not appear to fit into its environment. All decoration should be pleasing and in harmony with everything around it. This applies to carpets, soft furnishings, ornaments, flowers and plants. So often one visits a home or sees a picture of some interior where so much seems to be added as an afterthought or because it is the thing to do. In such surroundings plants will look out of place. They are too large for their position, too high for their comfort or, most prevalent, too isolated.

A plant should belong to a room. In spite of the fact that some people refer to plants as "contemporary" they are in fact timeless. There is not a setting that they will not grace so long as they are not out of proportion and so long as they are helped by the choice of the right accessories to fit into the scene. I have known people go to immense trouble to find the right vases for their flower arrangements so that they appear an integral part of the home decoration and yet those same people take a plant and dump it inside a large bowl much too wide and much too shallow so that the resulting ensemble is incongruous to a degree.

All flower pots are provided with a drainage hole in the base. Even if the pot is taken away to be watered and allowed to drain a certain amount of moisture will always seep through and so mark furniture, sill or floor on which the plant is stood. There are few things which make me feel quite so uncomfortable as a picture of a plant with no saucer, no pot container, no nothing, as some people would say. Magazines are the greatest defaulters in this respect and one feels that the photographer or art editor has decided that what is needed to give the shot a modern touch is a "contemporary" plant. Someone is sent to buy it and in it goes to provide "atmosphere" to the picture. If it is true that the public learn from advertisements then I fear that too many people are learning the wrong methods of displaying their plants.

Where a pot is not sunk in another container saucers are essential. In the first place they make for more efficient watering. Briefly, when the water is poured in the top of the pot it often courses right through the soil and flows out in the saucer. It should be allowed to remain there so that the pot may take it back again. Unless this is done the plant seldom gets sufficient moisture at one watering. In some cases, as I have already indicated, the plant flourishes best if a little water is actually allowed to remain in the saucer all the time.

Generally speaking I advocate the use of a container to protect the flower pot, as I shall explain later, but one may make an exception in the case of plants which prefer a drier condition from the others, geraniums, peperomias, sansevieria are examples. If however, they are to be set inside a deep container choose one sufficiently large to provide an air space between the pot and the container.

Flower pot saucers need not be dull. Indeed there are some lovely contemporary designs available nowadays. They are so attractive that a sill full of saucers designed by the same potter can be a very attractive area of the room. One imagines a sunny window full of mixed geraniums with the saucers glazed in the same hues of red. Visit a local pottery and see if you can get something made to fit your home.

Although they serve the purpose I cannot enthuse over the usual mixed bag of odd tea-set saucers one sees so often. Much more attractive than these, and costing very little, are the attractive pottery soup or cereal dishes. These will take a 60 or a 48 pot. The clean yellow, green, blue or shining brown look good with the plants. Take a look round the hardware store before deciding what saucers to buy, you are sure to find something unexpectedly suitable for your home.

If you prefer the more earthy touch you can buy terra-cotta flower pot saucers from any ironmonger or garden shop. These are glazed inside for, obviously, it is important that no moisture escapes. These saucers may be painted on the outside (although flower pots should never be in case injurious ingredients or fumes injure the plant). I have seen them banded in green and white, painted blue with white spots to match the curtains, and once just spotted colours over the natural fabric.

Recently I have seen some delightful Scandinavian flower pots complete with saucer. The flower pot itself is glazed and coloured but the interior is unglazed and there is a drainage hole. The colours are most pleasing and there are several combinations of hues. The pots too are in several sizes.

At one time experts recommended that glazed flower pots should not be used under any circumstances. (Some still maintain that this is so but opinions have changed). I give details later, but first of all just a word or two about the humble flower pot itself. Basically, it is good. Lines, texture and, to me at least, its colour is pleasing. This being so one asks, why not leave it as it is? Why cover it up with another pot? First we should ask ourselves why such soil containers as flower pots are in use universally and why they have been in use so long. The fact is that the pot is the nearest thing we can get to a piece of isolated earth in which to grow things. It is made of special earth clay and after manufacture takes on an essential porosity.

One might even say that the manufactured pot, like the earth from which it originates, breathes. How near to soil the finished pot is can be seen from the fact that certain humble plant organisms which are by no means choosy, will even grow on it. Indeed from the quantity of these minute growths on the outside of a flower pot one can often get guidance on how a special plant should be treated. For example, if the pot is very green from the covering of algae then it is pretty certain that the plant has been grown in a warm wet house.

In one way the pot is a little like the plant itself. From the pores through which it breathes it also gives off moisture. There's the rub. Often a flower pot which has no outer covering just gives off too much moisture altogether. You will find that where you have plain pots merely standing in a saucer you must watch the water situation very carefully. In hot dry conditions they can dry out even overnight.

That same porosity will enable the pot to take in a very limited amount of moisture. Indeed we might even say that the denseness of the pot controls the intake which fortunately is slower than the output. We can employ this factor to our advantage. A flower pot slipped inside another container will not dry out so quickly as one which stands with its entire surface exposed to evaporation.

As I was writing the last sentence I realized that my *Begonia rex* plants of which I wrote in the previous chapter are all standing inside other containers. This means that the only evaporation taking place is from the small surface of soil and the leaves. This may explain why I can grow them well yet keep them watered less frequently than is usually recommended.

Actually it is because plants generally do so much better when they are "plunged" that we are able to fit them so attractively into the home. There are containers galore. Not many of them perhaps were designed to take plants but one finds they are perfect for the purpose. My mind recalls for example an old foot bath, a large brown mixing bowl, a tall oven jar, many flower vases, a long wine cooler, a copper kettle, a metal log basket, a converted lampshade, a spice chest and a work box.

Many of my plants just fit into the rim of several vases I have and I find this a most attractive way of displaying them. My favourites are the china and pottery urns which can be bought almost everywhere. I have already told how attractive the spathiphyllum looks. The urns come in many colours but one design in black or white I have found most suitable. Some of the white ones I colour with an ordinary tempera water paint so that they harmonize with their setting or with the plant they hold. Try for example, a lilac tinted urn with a magenta slashed *Calathea oppenheima* and see how effective this is, or more simply a "silver" tradescantia in a lilac urn and a "golden" kind in a daffodil yellow vase. You can of course, should you wish, colour them permanently with plastic paint.

All white vases look very attractive with variegated plants. The classical black urns look well with the more sombre hued plants, especially those with a vestige of deep red or purple in their colourings such as the wonderful wine-red dracaenas although green and white plants look very effective in them. I have lately divided the variegated aspidistra and set a plant in a black urn.

Bronze urns or tall brown casseroles and copper jelly moulds look well with the mahogany spotted maranta. One lovely, almost globular deep brown bowl which I have used in the past for flowers just takes a 48 pot of *Begonia rex*. The pot rim rests tightly in the bowl which I have filled with crumbled used Florapak. This Florapak holds and retains any moisture that seeps through the drainage hole of the pot after watering and allows it to be taken back into the pot. More important still is that as long as the Florapak is slightly damp the plant does not dry out.

This brings me to an important point which explains why or how it is possible to grow a collection of plants in a warm dry room. If we can pack some kind of water retentive medium round a plant we can prevent the plant from quickly losing its moisture. Thus the plant benefits, but we benefit also for a plant grown this way does not need such constant care. Indeed once we can judge how quickly a particular plant uses its water supply we can in fact control it to a certain simple point. We can reach that desirable state where we can water say, once a week, fortnight or month according to what we grow and where we grow it.

It follows then that one should choose a container which is wider in diameter and deeper than the pot if this is possible, for it is best that there should be space all round the flower pot so that it may be well and truly plunged.

There are several kinds of materials which may be used. The choice is entirely up to you. Some will be easier to get locally than others. There is Florapak already mentioned. This is sold as a stem holder for flower arrangement. For plants either used Florapak may be used again or a new lump, bought from any florist, may be soaked, broken apart by the fingers into convenient lumps and packed under and around the pot. Peat is good especially for peat-loving plants such as azaleas. Saintpaulias appear to do better plunged into damp crumbled peat than they do isolated.

Horticultural peat may be bought at any garden shop. If too dry it is difficult and messy to use and it gives far less trouble if it is damped down first. A good test for correct dampness is that the peat should hold together when a handful is squeezed.

Easy to use is spaghnum or bog moss. This is a sponge-like moss, brownish rather than green. Once damp it holds water well. Because of this it is used by orchid growers in composts. In some districts it is easier to buy than others but once again one should be able to buy it in any good garden store.

Vermiculite is good and clean but is a little light and may blow about in an air current. This is not likely to happen if it is only in a small container, but it might if a larger area, a trough for example, is exposed to a draught. Mix it with agricultural sand to prevent this.

Pebbles or shingle are good, clean and I think, attractive. The only drawback is that they are weighty—a fact one has to take into consideration or it becomes impossible to move a large container. In some cases the weight might even cause a trough to give way should it not be constructed properly.

There is the same objection to the use of sand. Incidentally you will notice that I have referred to agricultural sand. This is silver or river sand. Builder's sand is cheaper but it can contain substances which might be harmful to plant life. One can usually buy a very small quantity, three pennyworth for example, at the ironmongers.

You may know of some other medium which will fulfil the same functions of any of these I have mentioned. The essentials are that these should contain no harmful substances, that they should hold, or rather retain, water and be clean to handle. When the pot is in position the level of this packing material should not come above the rim of the pot.

If the pot is to be sunk into a container of which the rim dimensions are only a little larger than its own so that a fairly tight fit results, and if the container is deeper than the pot, a layer of packing material should first be placed in the container. No vacuum should be allowed to form, otherwise water will collect in this empty space, the level growing higher all the time until one day the base of the pot will be in water. If this is unnoticed the plant can easily die. Should pots be set in containers of this kind that have no packing material in them, they should be inspected after watering and any surplus poured away.

Obviously, the container, if a tall one, should be large enough. A few bare inches of flower pot protruding above the rim of a container can look very ugly.

This method of sinking a flower pot into another container is, of course, not a long step from plunging a whole collection of plants in a trough or other indoor garden. But before I go into more details on this subject a few more points about individual containers.

An important point in favour of the use of tall vases as pot containers is that the plant is raised, given additional height. It has more chance to show off its beauty. The height gained throws the shape into silhouette and allows space underneath the lower leaves and branches which adds greatly to the general attractiveness and importance of the arrangement. In some cases there is almost a transformation.

A hydrangea, for example, is often somewhat stumpy, but if one unloosens some of the restricting ties, and even takes away the centre stake, and then allows the plant to fall more naturally it becomes every bit as graceful as an arrangement of cut stems.

One rule though that results in good proportions is—the container into which the pot is sunk needs to be as high as the plant itself.

Nowadays plant containers are legion. They are a far cry from the art pots of the '30s. There are pottery, plastic, wrought iron, metal mesh, wicker work and sometimes a combination of say a wicker cage holding a glazed pot. I use and like the various pots, particularly a tall container that takes a large 60. Any ivy trailing over this rough grey surface looks most effective. Indeed I can find nothing but praise for most containers designed by potters. There is room for the pot and room for the water. But not all containers are as practical nor as lovely.

Greatest offenders in my eyes are some of the metal plant holders designed to be fixed or to hang on walls. I feel that some of these must have been designed by people who have never grown plants. As a rule these holders are complete with a little metal saucer. One sets the plant in place with the pot base in the saucer—if it will go in! Usually the saucer has been made so small that the pot has to be forced into it. But this is no good! Watering will have to be done so carefully that either the plant will never get sufficient at one go and you will have to stand over it giving it drop by drop or else, because there is not quick enough suction to pull the water down rapidly it will trickle over

All kinds of vessels may be used as plant containers whether the pots are plunged into them or they are actually planted. Holding fern, coleus, peperomia, tradescantia and ivies, is an old white china foot-bath. The plant on the left is *Sansevieria trifasciata*.

A well lit alcove built over an old fireplace is an ideal place to grow or propagate slightly tender plants. The bowl in the centre holds germinating avocado pear stones. On the left and to the right of a french window is *Cissus antarctica*. The tripod cone pot on the right may be moved about when the heat is on, or the sun too bright. *Scindapsus aureus* on the left dislikes intensely any sunlight on its leaves. Hyacinth bulbs in the bowl are growing in pebbles and water, and have just been brought into the light from a dark, cool cupboard.

Plants grow towards the light. Placed on a wall opposite the window
they show at their best. *Ficus pumila* on the right needs a lot of water:
once shrivelled it will never revive. Immerse the pot weekly.

Right: Three hyacinths can be more than just three bulb plants to a pot. Here they have been mixed with a little ivy on the left and tradescantia on the right, both have been planted in the bulb fibre. Among the plants two or three small tablet tubes are pressed down in the fibre, filled with water to hold small posies of spring flowers. *Below:* The grapevine ivy, *Rhoicissus*, will live in the same pot for years, but to be most effective it needs supporting. The plant becomes more attractive as it matures.

the rim of the pot and cascade down the wall leaving a nasty stain!

There needs to be at least a quarter inch margin all round between the base of the pot and the rim of the saucer. Unfortunately I once bought various examples of these metal holders and had to substitute a small bowl. Fortunately trailing plants soon hide the container.

A good thing though about many metal holders is the way they have been designed to hang perfectly straight on the wall. Some have a fan of metal behind the pot. This is formed in a variety of ways, angled or looped or zig-zagged. Not only does it ensure that the pot is firmly held but the parts of the fan provide ready-made and attractive supports for stems. One needs only to hook a trail or an upright branch as one wishes without resorting to an ungainly stiff cane.

Some of these holders are made to carry more than one pot which allows for an attractive variation in a wall decoration. Incidentally see that none of them is hung too high for the comfort of the plants and for your own convenience when watering.

Not all metal holders are designed for wall use. Some are shaped like troughs, some are round tables edged so that plants may be massed inside. In fact there is infinite variety. Much depends on personal taste and on the furnishing of your house. One thing though to be considered is that all these things have to be dusted and will often be wet owing to spraying and watering so there should be no danger of rusting.

Wicker plant holders are numerous. They are mainly practical and pleasing, harmonizing well with plant material. Some of these are provided with metal, terra-cotta or pottery drip pans but others have none.

In most cases, particularly where the wicker is pliable it is a simple matter to bend the bars out of shape while drip pan or pot is being set inside. The "champagne" bottle basket is an example, one pushes it downwards from the top and through the wider spaces made this way insert the pot.

Our Old Glory is in one of these bottle holders. This had a deep tin lining (incidentally some empty food tins are just the right size and depth for linings). Recently I noticed that this had begun to rust and that there was danger of it springing a leak. Fortunately a small cheap sugar basin fits well and was an easy replacement. Although such things as cake tins, patty pans and even the foil saucers sold for food containers, are cheap and convenient to use, I always try to substitute something less likely to rust.

Sometimes the plant holders designed to hang on a wall do not hang as well as they should once the plant is placed in them. It is important that the top of the pot be level so that watering doesn't result in stained walls and carpets. A piece of cork stuck to the back of the holder may be used to adjust the angle. This will not mark the wall.

In summer when I know that drying off will be rapid I take any large permanent wicker plant arrangement and plunge the whole thing in a bucket of water. While the soil is bubbling away letting out the air and taking in the water I spray the leaves and gently scrub down the wicker. Even plain water will remove most of the dust and grime. Rain water is better. One should take care that the whole ensemble is well drained before attempting to replace it. If you stand it on a pad of newspaper the surplus moisture will soon be drained off.

If you wish to renew any kind of plant holder with a coat of paint, the plant must be removed and set well out of the way, for paint fumes have been known to kill plants.

Now a word about the arrangements in large containers or troughs, window-boxes, log chests, outsize baskets or whatever you will. These may be done in two ways and I shall explain the method of plunging them in detail in a coming chapter. As I said earlier it is possible to buy metal troughs which can be used as indoor window-boxes. Examine them carefully though before making a selection for once again, some of those made of metal mesh have a drip tray which is really much too shallow to be of much use. It needs to be at least an inch deep. See also that the trough itself is deep enough to hide the pot rim. If the pots are to be plunged in a trough with solid walls there needs to be at least an inch to spare so that the pot can be stood on a layer of medium and still not protrude above the top of the trough.

For 60 pots long troughs usually for flower arrangement will fit neatly along most window-sills. These may be in metal or pottery. They will take two or three pots.

There are some extremely attractive troughs in green, white or wine surrounded by a detachable metal frame of copper or white scrolled wire. Two or more of these according to the space available, will fit on most window-sills quite safely. They are ideal to hold non-trailing plants for they are attractive yet do not detract from the plant.

Plastic square kitchen bowls come in a gay range of colours. Two or more set on a rectangular coffee table before a window will give you a clean, easily moved, easily made indoor window-box. This way too the plants may be isolated according to their likes. Cactus and succulents in one, paddlers in another, and normal beings in another. Try scarlet and all red hues in a red bowl, yellow variegated plants in a yellow bowl, and vines and amethysts in a blue bowl.

Some troughs, and there are all sizes in all kinds of wood and other materials, are legged. Besides looking attractive they are extremely practical. In the first place it is so easy to dust under them. Secondly evaporation can take place under them so if by chance any water should seep out there is no fear of them becoming mildewed and thirdly one can move the plants around a little to their advantage. One can, for example take them to a sunny window in winter when there is little danger of sunburn or one can easily move the trough away or to the side of the window in summer.

In winter one can draw the curtains and bring the plant into the room. Incidentally, no plant should be left on a sill or on the wrong side of the curtains during a cold spell. This is where the temperature of the room falls most. Bring the plants into the warm and light of the room. They will enjoy it and will live longer and you will enjoy their company. It seems contradictory to buy a plant for its beauty and to hide it away during the time of day when one is most likely to have the leisure to appreciate its good points.

If you cannot find just the trough you want it is possible to have one made to measure. Covered with an attractive laminate troughs may be made part of the furnishings. Have a tin-smith make linings for you or have them treated with pitch inside.

If for some reasons troughs or large plunger window-boxes are out of the question you can easily establish water-tight trays tailored to fit any sill. How deep they are will depend on you, but one should allow for a good layer of pebbles which can be kept constantly moist. The pots may be sunk into these even if only for the depth of an inch or two. The ideal would be, of course, seven inches deep so as to hide any pot. If these trays were painted to match the window-frame the effect would be most pleasing.

For bright splashes of colour among the permanent foliage plants, set impatiens, begonias (winter and summer), gloxinias, cyclamen and primulas. All these will do well on the damp pebbles. Here the plants could be changed as required without causing too much mess or inconvenience—pebbles are easily picked up should a few fall.

Remember to turn the pots daily to ensure even growth. Legged troughs and similar containers can be turned entire so that individual pots need not be disturbed.

Simpler than the troughs, for some are designed to take only one plant, are the cone shaped containers set into a metal tripod. I have three of these made in plastic, green, yellow and red. In the green is an aspidistra whose leaves are much brighter and sharper than the blue-green of the plastic, the yellow one takes a tall green and yellow sansevieria, and the red one rests on the floor with a holly ivy in it.

These are obtainable also in terra-cotta and some are large enough to be miniature gardens. I should like one very much, and perhaps when my co-editing husband reads through this text he will take note of this fact. (Maybe by the time the book goes to press I shall have it.) (She has!)

So much depends on the type of house you live in of course, but if they are suitable, the wicker washing-basket, lidless hamper, rush basket or log carrier are all delightful containers providing, as one would expect from such natural materials, the right atmosphere for the pattern of leaf and stem. Plants can be plunged or planted in these. I find that the best means of keeping the moisture inside them is to line them with linen— an old shirt is just the thing! Obviously they are not so durable as copper or china so they must not be allowed to rot. They should be given a chance to dry out occasionally.

One most useful container I have is an old white footbath deep enough to take a 32 pot should that be necessary. Smaller pots are hoisted up to rim level by standing them on a little pile of upturned pots of the same size.

Copper preserving-pans, and any of those deep metal vessels that so many of us collect, will hold several pots (remember that it may be too heavy to carry when filled). I have three Benares bowls, two brass, one copper. I bought them for a song and for the beauty of their metal rather than their shape and usefulness but I must say that now each contains a plant, one a giant *Ficus decora* I cannot imagine ever dispensing with them. There is ample room for the crumbled Florapak I use as a filling and the pot fits in neatly yet not tightly just below rim level. They suit the cottage where since the rooms are low, they stand on the floor silhouetted against the wall.

The floor in fact is often the best level for some plants. One has the opportunity of looking down on the leaves and so seeing them at their best. The pot is not too obvious in this position either. Really big plants, such as monstera, *Philodendron bipinnatifidum*, and some ficus look ungainly if staged off the floor.

All these containers I have mentioned are fairly straight-forward and are not likely to raise any passions in any breast. What does arouse controversy is the affirmation by people like myself that plants can be grown in soup tureens, shiny bulb bowls, copper pans, teapots or similar vessels that have no drainage holes. There is a school of horticulturists who affirm that where there is no drainage hole there cannot be a happy plant. Once again I must beg to differ.

Before me as I write there sits on the table near the window a plant arrangement consisting of a *Peperomia hederafolia*, tradescantia and hedera. It is flourishing and has grown con-siderably since it was first planted. The peperomia has even flowered. New leaves abound. It has a little story. A firm of glass and pottery exporters showed the container to my husband and told him that it did not sell because people could not visualize plants growing in it. My husband persuaded them to let me plant it, which I did. The interesting thing is this. At the time of planting I bought three peperomias, one large and two small. These need little water. Unfortunately a member of my household on two or three occasions noticing that the two iso-lated specimens (in drained pots by the way) were dry, gave them good drinks. They are now most unhappy and are con-valescing in the bedroom where I have a small sick bay. But the little fellow that was made to share a home with two other plants in a non-drained container is most healthy.

Three years ago I visited a clever geranium grower who was

kind enough to give me a plant of the purple, cream and green ivy-leaved *Pelargonium l'elegante*. This was in a flower pot and I had it photographed. Shortly after I transferred it to a white fluted bowl with a shiny green interior. In this the plant has not only grown but thrived and considerably increased. It has been joined by cuttings of tradescantia and all plants have got well away. For the first year the pelargonium hardly moved, but it was significant that it did not go back in any way. In the autumn of 1956 however, it showed a great improvement, first one new shoot started to grow and is now towering above all the older growth. Meanwhile two new shoots are trying to catch up. All this in a shiny bowl with no drainage. We are always told that geraniums must be sharply drained. So mine is, but not by holes. A drainage system is established so that the water must pass quickly through the soil. Aeration must take place. For this I have provided and obviously it works.

I can quote other examples for they are here all around me. I once saw a terra-cotta pitcher in which an ivy had been growing—and thriving—for years.

There are though certain principles which must always be observed. Fortunately they are simple ones and I am going into them in great detail presently. The purpose of mentioning them here is to impress on you that if you have suitable dishes or bowls or if you can buy any cheaply then they may be used. You will find that the plants look very pretty growing in them. They seem to sprawl more at ease than they do in a pot. I would never use an ordinary pot if I could use a more attractive dish which, after all, is more likely to look more at home in my room.

If you are an enthusiast for sales keep an eye open for large earthenware pots constructed on the strawberry barrel design. These will have pockets made about their surface. The idea is that plants are set in these and also planted in the top in considerable variety. Use cascading or trailing plants for the sides and stiffer leaved specimens for the top. A local potter would make you a similar pot if you described it I am sure.

At the same sales look out for stone ornaments of the gargoyle type, stone troughs, vases and even pickling jars, if your rooms are big enough to use them.

So my last piece of advice in this chapter is never to take anything at face value, particularly where containers are concerned. If you have something in which you think plants would look good, go ahead and try it out. If on the other hand you need to buy containers don't choose expensive things specially made to hold plants until you have wandered round and had a quiet search in the china department, hardware and junk store.

CHAPTER FIVE

HELPING THEM TO LOOK THEIR BEST

WHEN we moved into our present Covent Garden flat
from the low ceilinged, cosy and colourful attic
around the corner, the tall Regency rooms looked
cold and standoffish. We felt that we had to provide the homely
touch and do it quickly. There was one thing we could do—
bring in some more plants in addition to those we had brought
with us on our move. So this we did. Now, after a year, each
week what I can only describe as the outlines of the home are
getting softer as a plant curves around this archway or stretches
over this wall to a window.

To newly-weds with purses too shallow for a real spending
spree or to a man or woman who wishes to make a bedsitter or
little flat look homelike, my advice always is to spend a couple
of pounds on a really large plant, or even two. Of course one
has to decide just how big it should be according to the space
it has to fill. This way one can quickly and attractively furnish
one side of a room, a corner or a window.

It is wise also to raise a few annual climbers like *Cobea
scandens*, the cup and saucer plant, or the heavenly Morning
Glories, *Ipomaea*, and to let them scramble around or even on to
a window. Raising such plants from a packet of seed, by the
way, is a grand compensation for having no garden. As one
fellow writer who works on a magazine said to me: "Flowers
live and die while you are away at the office, but if you grow a
plant or two you can note its progress each night when you get
home. It's like coming home to a pal."

There is such a lot we would like to do to our rooms, but as we are so busy when in town and as we are fortunate enough to have our feet in the country, as it were, with a huge garden to tend at weekends, there never seems enough time to get a tenth of it done. But once again we find that plants help us out. Let me explain.

In the office is a fireplace and mantelpiece, quite plain but large. It is not practical to have an open fire in the winter and in any case we are anti-smog and try to keep from adding to the already sooty atmosphere of London. So the hearth has been boarded up and we hope one day to turn this space into a filing cabinet and so conceal for ever the fact that it was once a fireplace. In the meantime its former purpose is obvious, so we try to distract attention from it. On the end of the mantel, say five feet from a very high window, we have a cluster of various ivies, their pots standing in a shallow rectangular dish which just fits the shelf and is inconspicuous.

One ivy, *H. ravenholst*, is five feet tall and it travels up parallel with the edge of the chimney piece and then strikes out horizontally when it hits the warmer air level about nine feet above the floor. It is very handsome. At its foot and hiding its pot and cascasing over the edge of the mantelpiece and again facing the window is a Chicago ivy. This has been grown in a 60 pot for years and is regularly fed a plant tablet which it both needs and enjoys. To the side of this and designed to provide contrast, is a *Hedera glacier*. This variety I find needs more water than Chicago although it is a hardier type. Sometimes I may need to water this twice a week to the other's once.

This little plant group serves its purpose as we intended it should. On entering the room visitors remark first on the ivies and I have not yet heard a comment on the blocked-in fireplace. I can assure you, too, that some visitors are sufficiently friendly to be quite brutal in their comments.

Elsewhere we have a piece of furniture which I find useful

but unpleasing in appearance. Until it can be replaced I try once again to divert attention from it. It faces the door and stands against the wall space between two windows. Over it hangs a mirror which catches and reflects quite a lot of light. Over this has been hung a plectranthus. This pretty, easy to grow plant really roams. I give trailing support by stretching white cotton from the mirror hook to the window frames. The trails rest on the cotton which is invisible until one is close to it. Altogether it presents such a graceful appearance that admiration for it and disregard for the furniture is always forthcoming I have noticed.

In the kitchen, although the window is good and large, the view is bleak. The sooty glass roof of a warehouse below is only too visible and the previous tenants of the flat overcame this obstacle by installing frosted glass in the window frame and so shutting off the view entirely. To my mind this is not only escapist, it is also claustrophobic. Something had to be done to arrest the eye before it travelled outside to that horrid roof. The wide wooden surround to the window has been painted red, which both matches other woodwork and also provides the natural complementary colour to green. The sill is covered with plastic material to match. On it stands a large small-leaved ivy which is encouraged to climb up and up.

The kitchen has been sliced off our living-room leaving it narrower than was originally intended and designed. We are fortunate in having at the end of this room a french-door leading on to a roof garden. At first we had a room divider at right angles to this door on which all kinds of plants were growing. But this was summer time and the room faces north. We realized that the situation was likely to prove too dark and cold for many of the plants in winter. So the room divider was moved elsewhere. But at the same time we had the woodwork, originally dark brown, painted a light apple green. As the room faces north, as light is so precious and as we are not overlooked, we decided to do without curtains. But the frame of the doorway looked too bare as it was.

It is here we grow our ten-foot-high ravenholst. It is in the corner, between wall and door. We chose this variety for several reasons. It is large leaved but hardier than, say, a *Ficus elastica*. We know that it approves of the general atmosphere in the flat. We know that we can depend on an ivy to put out those delightful frivolous little frills and trails which are just what is needed to offset the severe lines of the doorway and window frame.

The plant was not too happy at first. It shed many of its leaves after they had turned yellow, but this was what we more or less expected, since we bought it in the fall of the year when the days were shortening and the light less powerful. To make matters worse the room fails to get any sun at all at this season. So the plant had to make some considerable effort to adjust itself to its new conditions. By February, though, the new trails were leaning out from the stiff pillar of main stems, new leaves were opening almost daily and the plant began at last to play the role we had intended for it. The trails, beside being decorative, helped it merge into its surroundings. The strict division of wall and plant was delightfully blended.

Keen flower arrangers have long appreciated the possibilities of using an arrangement not merely as an ornament but as a useful part of design. Long, low arrangements are placed in rooms that are too high, the length of the arrangement so positioned as to suggest the width which is lacking. A vividly coloured arrangement might be placed at the end of a room which is too wide or perhaps arranged to draw the eye down the room and take in some particular feature.

One can do exactly the same thing with plants but to a greater extent. Once in place, plants will not have to be renewed so frequently as fresh flowers. If you have a room that is too narrow, then fix a plant so that it trails swag-like across one of the narrow ends. The pot need not be dead centre, indeed, you will often get a more pleasing effect if it is a little to one side.

Remember that because they are living, plants bring a warm touch to their surroundings. A large hall, light but echoing, is likely to have a certain chill atmosphere about it, but one or two large plants placed where the leaves can catch the sun and throw dappled shadows on the wall will make a world of difference.

Where one wall of a hall or room is mainly glass, a window box on each side of the door will lend enchantment. The contents can be varied according to the seasons. One could, for example, see that there were permanent plants (perhaps rhoicissus, ivy, ficus or cissus) flanking the door and a trailer falling over the far edge (say tradescantia, plectranthus, peperomia or hedera) and another in the centre climbing and trailing. In spring these could be contrasted with pots of hyacinths, daffodils or tulips, to be followed with cinerarias or primulas; in summer, succeeded by annuals in pots, begonias or gloxinias and in autumn, michaelmas daisies (yes, in pots: the dwarf varieties are ideal for this purpose), terminating with chrysanthemums, cyclamen or orange berried solanums.

This is just one suggestion, of course, to show what can be done. Individual requirements may demand that less time or money is spent on such a decorative feature. It is quite easy to fill the boxes with permanent plants and still have great variety.

There have been so many pictures published showing the use of living plants as screens and backgrounds that there is now nothing original in the suggestion. Original or not, the suggestion still has its uses. As a rule a trough is filled with climbing plants and stakes or string are provided at intervals so that plant trails may climb and so screen or cover the required area. But so often this result requires a softening touch, I find. Although one wishes the plants to grow upwards, one should remember at the same time that the trough or other container also needs some screening. Plants set in this fashion will grow so that they face the light, so one should ensure that the stakes or supports are fixed at the back and not in the centre. This gives plenty of room for the climbing plants to grow and face the light and for the cover plants to increase. These are much more likely to find their way over the edge than to scramble over the soil surface.

If it does not spoil the effect sought after and if it can be arranged physically, it is often a good plan to have one or more plants suspended half-way up the screen. Perhaps it may be fixed on the wall, if one adjoins, or perhaps a shelf made of a few bamboos lashed to those which form the screen. This suspended plant may be left to trail downwards as it wishes rather than be trained to climb. It will provide mass and interest where the other plants are at their thinnest. "Angles" can be created this way and if a similar yet contrasting plant is used the effect can be most pleasing. For example, a screen consisting of the dainty green and white *Hedera glacier* could have a top left corner and lower right section of *Hedera sagittifolia*, a species with arrow shaped leaves (as the name tells us) and a dense habit. This plant grows strongly and thickly and if left unsupported the stems spiral and curve very prettily.

An empty corner can be quickly and most attractively furnished with plants. Extra light and extra decorative effect can be gained by hanging a mirror so as to reflect the window light. All kinds of stands may be used to build a display, but one must keep in mind the fact that the plant pots must always be accessible for watering, for too often a difficult-to-get-at pot is neglected with consequent damage to the plant. An old what-not, a corner cupboard, a spice cupboard or one of those corner fitments used in modern kitchens with three corner shelves, all can form the foundation. Tall, tree-like plants such as some of the ficus family can be made to tower above the others and to give shade to those that enjoy it.

Don't hesitate to bring in a few plants from out of doors if you have a garden or the opportunity to obtain them elsewhere. I have already mentioned a fatsia. It makes a most exotic look-ing indoor plant with glossy, green, palmate leaves not unlike those of a fig tree. These plants can be bought ready potted as room plants. They are perhaps inclined to tire easily and require frequent re-potting or they drop their leaves.

Also unexpectedly effective when potted and set in an attrac-tive holder is the spotted laurel or aucuba. Little plants of these may be bought ready potted and will last some weeks in an indoor window box and longer still, of course, if planted out of doors.

One spring I cheated and brought blossom to the plant corner in my bedroom in London. I picked a long branch of plum, stood it on the floor in a tall heavy vase and let it grow up and bloom among the sharp outlines and the severe greens of the house plants.

A fine piece of pottery or some ornament of which you are proud can be limelighted by a plant or two. The stems may be arranged forming a frame, to accentuate a colour or a shape or the plant may be selected for its contrast value.

Writing of using a plant or part of it as a frame reminds me that plants as they come from nursery or shop are too stiffly tied and supported to be used as drapes. It interests me to see that while few people, if any, would dream of placing in a vase a bunch of flowers just as it comes from the florist shop, the same people seldom seem to realize that a plant too is bunched. True, there will be many plants that need no more than a little coaxing into more attractive shapes. These are plants such as azaleas, solanums, ferns, some peperomias, marantas and others that do not need staking or tying to bring them into compact shape.

Sometimes, as this might well apply even to some of the plants mentioned above, the nurseryman or florist ties a raffia or tape support around the underpart of the leaves or branches, thus bringing them upwards and so protecting the blooms or the young shoots at the centre. Tied this way the plant is easier to wrap. Obviously this tie must be loosened and the plant restored to its original and natural form as soon as possible. Sometimes the plant, especially azaleas and genistas, assume a better shape if the lower branches are coaxed downwards a little.

If you buy any kind of trailing or climbing plant (except for the very small and immature sizes) you will find that all the trails have been gathered up and grow supported by a central stake. This gives a bushy plant and serves the further purpose of protecting the young tips during the arduous processes of marketing. Unless you have a definite reason for wishing to grow a thick pillar of green it is advisable to loosen the plant before it is set in place. First give it its welcome drink, for it is much easier to plunge a tidy plant in a bucket than a loosely trailing one.

Next decide what purpose it is to serve and where it is to go. Have ready, too, what supports you intend to use, for it is not a good thing to let heavy branches flop around. They may become damaged. Sometimes the plant is ungainly or wrongly shaped or your purpose. If it offends me I never hesitate to cut away a branch from azalea, solanum, genista or any other such bush.

Often the plant's own leaves will support the flowers. The heart shaped foliage of cyclamen, for example, may be cupped around a stem which appears to want to flop too far over in one direction. Cyclamen flowers are inclined to cluster together. Separated, and each given a leaf to hold it in place, they give greater colour value and the opportunity to see more clearly each pretty flower.

There are many kinds of artificial supports you can use for your plants. First consider painting an ordinary cane to match

A corner for plants could be found in many rooms and a plastic linoleum or tiled top is easily wiped down: even so all plants are best stood in saucers or pot containers to protect surfaces they stand on.

Above, left: A blue-green bromeliad tones with the "bloom" on the bronze pot. *Above, right:* Plants are actually growing in the metal container. The central dracaena is ruby red: blue-green peperomia below it, with silver and green trailing plants. *Below, left:* A columnea studded with scarlet flowers is held high in the bowl of a copper lamp standard. *Below, right:* Silver Queen scindapsus, purple and silver *Begonia rex;* yellow, green and grey sansevieria, and blue-grey peperomia, which fit well in modern settings with bright colours and sharply defined forms.

the wall before which the plant is to stand. All plants are not going to be trained along a wall. Some will be attached to a main support, yet allowed to fall away from it as naturally as possible. It is not a good thing to cut the stake level with the top of the plant because if it enjoys its environment the plant will soon race away above its support. Much better to have a stout support which seems too tall for its purpose. If this is painted as I suggest, it will not be too conspicuous.

Often the original stake is neither strong nor long enough for later growth and, rather than pull the plant about once it is established, it is better to change the stake in its earliest days.

There are some useful transparent plastic supports which may be bought from the florist. These are from about two feet long, straight or curved. They are ideal for setting in the pot at an angle and as they are twisted, corkscrew fashion, a stem can be twined around them and held securely in the curves.

Some people with imagination and capable fingers can make more unusual plant supports. Wicker can be soaked and coaxed into various shapes. Two hearts entwined can be attractive without being coy; a long cane or wire serpent can climb close to a wall; five or seven slender canes set fanwise form a solid yet not dense frame; five canes, their bases set round the side of the pot, hooped and fastened in a top knot, set the foundation for a globe of green; a concertina made from a strip of wire mesh with a cane threaded down the centre for support and easy fixing, the lot painted to match the wall, is ideal for plants with delicate trails like *Cissus sicyoides* and some hederas.

If you wish to have a stem trailing across a wall there are various ways in which they may be anchored. Transparent tape is good if the wall is not papered, but it is apt to take any paper away with it when it is removed. On a papered wall an ordinary pin is quite efficient, surprisingly strong and really not very easy to see. The pin should be pushed in at an angle and the

97

stem just draped over it. Little green paper loops and thumb tacks can be used if you have a wall that will take the tacks— some modern walls are too hard. Hook the stem with the paper (folded wrapping paper in strips one inch by a quarter will do for all but very thick stems), place the two ends together above the stem and push the tack through them into the wall. If this fastening is made near a leaf it can be hidden from view.

I find cotton, white or wall matching, extremely strong and useful. This I attach to the pot holder, or if this is not possible, to the base of the stem. A length is then extended in whatever direction I wish the growth to travel, and secured. Usually a small loop and a thumb tack are sufficient. The trail is laid along this and, unless it is being trained to a new angle, surprisingly it stays put.

Wishing to train a heavy stem of *Cissus antarctica*, I used very fine reel wire, thinking that the cotton might not be strong enough. This proved to be almost embarrassingly inconspicuous, for when the time came to move the plant I had some difficulty in locating the wire.

One should take care when fastening a stem to a support that the fastening is not made too tight or the stem might become strangled, in which case it will probably die. Most nurserymen use wire rings, either plain or green. The hoop or ring is merely opened to embrace the stem and support and then allowed to spring back into shape. Usually one can find enough of those remaining low on a plant stem where they no longer serve a purpose. They can be opened up, taken off and used on a more necessary part of the stem.

Alternatively, green paper covered wires, or brown pipe cleaners (cut in half if they are too long) may also be used. The important points are that a support, clip or tie should be as inconspicuous as possible, easy to apply and easy to remove. Inspect the plants occasionally to make sure that ties are not too tight if the stems have thickened.

Tie between leaves. Never tie a leaf to a stem, for this should remain free to grow to the light as it needs.

Before unloosening a new plant, decide just where it is to go and what role it is to play. If it is to stand upright, then obviously it will be neither necessary nor desirable to loosen the growths down to soil level. But one or two tips should be released so that they fall away a little from the main stem.

The support on a thick single stemmed plant such as *Ficus decora, F. elastica* or *Monstera deliciosa*, may be left as it is unless you find it too unsightly. If you remove any stake supporting a main stem, watch the end of the cane as it is taken out. It is frequently all too easy to let it come into contact with the young growing tip of the plant and so cause irreparable damage.

For plants that are to trail or climb, first set them in position. Unless you do this you can have no idea how much of the plant pot needs to be screened, nor if the plant as it stands is too tall, too high in the room or too bulky for its position.

Next decide what is to be the main flow of the plant. Do you want it to move to the left, right, upwards, downwards or perpendicularly? Decide these things and then set the supports in place if they are to be used. Unloose the plant from the top downwards.

Study the stems or trails of the plant so that if there is one that naturally falls to the right, it can be arranged in that direction. Try not to have stems crossing each other at first. If they want to grow that way later on they will and in a much more attractive manner than we can devise. For although a little artifice is permissible, indeed essential, the natural desires of the plants should not be thwarted entirely. It is, after all, the natural habit of growth of these plants that makes them attractive to us.

The question of aspect is a very important one. People with good windows, mainly facing west and south, will have little to worry over. They can grow any kind of plant, putting those like geraniums which like to be baked directly in the window and setting others a little farther back according to their needs.

Sunny rooms, even without plants, have life brought to them by the light alone. Plants emphasize this lively note, but how much more are they needed in the comparatively lifeless atmosphere of rooms which face north or east. Unfortunately these aspects bring their own problems. Some plants are not happy with such low light intensity as daylight alone brings. If artificial light is used most of the day the problem is not so acute. But although constant use of this light is the rule in many offices, it is certainly the exception at home.

Fortunately some plants can stand little light, although they may grow and develop more slowly than they would under lighter conditions. These include all ferns, ivies, *Scindapsus aureus* and varieties, tradescantia, aspidistra, chlorophytum, dieffenbachia, ficus of all kinds, philodendrons, *Rhoicissus rhomboidea*, sansevieria.

As a general rule do not expect good performance and certainly not a lavish show of bloom from plants that like very dry sunny conditions. These include geraniums, flowering cacti and bryophyllums.

If I may make a suggestion, even though they do well in north facing rooms, avoid a heavy use of large dark green leaved plants. An impression of light is more likely to be given by using *Ficus elastica variegata*, variegated ivies and any yellow or white slashed plant. The variegated aspidistra is particularly effective. At the same time, avoid dark containers.

CHAPTER SIX

GOOD COMPANIONS FOR
PLANT COMMUNITIES

I N THEIR native state plants grow in communities. What might at first sight appear to be a mass of one kind or species proves on closer inspection to be a harmonious mixture. Ecologists realize that such mixtures are not haphazard. The health of each plant appears to be dependent on certain conditions, often created by one or more of the other members of the community. For example, bluebells enjoy not only the special light conditions which exist in a beech wood, but also the rich spongy top layers of leaf mould formed by the annual fall.

Although some of my mixtures may not be ecologically scientific, I like to see one plant rubbing shoulders with another indoors. In fact, because I am not a scientist I am ruled by the heart instead of the brain. For this reason I use plants that contrast with or complement each other—no hard task with such a range to choose from. This way the beauty of sharp and sculpted forms is enhanced by soft clinging trails. Shining leaves may be contrasted with soft, downy foliage, bare stems with a mass of leaves.

When arranging a window-box or trough or some similar community, remember that a variety of shapes and characters will give a more attractive result than if all the plants are of the same kind. For example, if all the plants grow formally and upright like the sansevieria or dracaena, the arrangement may look too stiff. But if some plants are selected that will cascade or trail over the edge of the container and others climb higher and so reach above the rest, the arrangement will have variety.

It might be cheaper and more convenient to buy six of one kind of plant and six of another. If so, see that they contrast. If six green and white grass-like chlorophytum are purchased, for example, dark leaved ivies or monsteras can be used to show both to best advantage.

As in a garden, all will blend with all so long as one studies the individual requirements of the plants and does not attempt the impossible. Obviously it is not a good thing to group together in one container plants that prefer a very dry soil such as a sansevieria and a primula that likes to be really moist at the roots. So long as these basic requirements are studied, I have no hesitation in mixing flowering plants, green plants, ferns, permanent shrubs and bulbs in any way that pleases me.

Elsewhere I have mentioned growing plants in bowls and tureens. You may be quite happy with your individual, isolated plants and have no desire to make a garden in miniature, but on the other hand, if you do take cuttings and so propagate the stock, you might like to know how to grow them on. These young plants may be mixed or left as individuals, but more of this later. You should also know how to re-pot a plant, for this is the operation on which all other planting is based.

Do not be in a hurry to re-pot. One man who grows literally millions of plants for market says that he is sure gardeners are much too impatient and want to move the plants along before they are ready for it. Speaking generally, I should say that from the time you first buy it until at least six months later is invariably a safe period to keep a plant in its original pot. There will always be sufficient plant foods in the compost to last that time. After this period I should begin giving the plant food in tablet, powder or liquid form about once a month, depending on the time of year and the state of growth.

Indications that the plant is pot-bound may be shown at any time after this original six month period but usually later rather than earlier. The most common symptom is that the mature leaves become smaller and smaller as they grow. Growth generally is not so vigorous as it was. Everything will be slowed down.

Do not confuse this slowing down with a natural resting period of the plant. You can make quite certain that the plant is root-bound by tipping out from the pot what is known as the root ball and examining it. This is quite simple to do and the root ball, looking a little like a very firm sand pie, can be replaced in the pot again without any damage having been done to it. Do not attempt to knock out an over-dry plant. Water it first and allow it to drain.

First you must hold the plant in position so that it does not become severed at the root. Place your right hand over the top of the pot with the stem portion coming up between the second and third fingers. Quickly turn the plant upside down and tap the edge of the pot on the edge of a table or on another pot. This will loosen the pot from the clinging soil and you will find that you can slide it off the root ball which will remain intact. Keep the plant upside down, still holding the plant with your fingers. If you find a mat of roots or many roots spiralling around at the base and more roots than soil, then the plant needs re-potting. Slip it back in the pot, making sure that it fits tightly without air space at the sides. Give it another sharp tap, this time on its base, to settle it back in position. Now you can make preparation for the transfer of the plant to a larger home.

However, it may be that a larger pot will not fit into your scheme of things. To change it would mean changing the plant holder too. In that case, let the plant remain in its small pot but water it rather more often and feed it regularly. Some liquid manure would be welcomed and dried blood, which can be bought quite conveniently, would provide helpful nourishment.

In a case like this it is also sometimes possible to replenish the soil from the top. Loosen the top soil in the pot as gently as possible, for you must take care not to damage the roots, and remove at least half an inch of top soil. If, or when, any roots become visible, stop work. Replace this soil with John Innes final potting compost. A handful of soil brought in from the garden is not quite the same for it is most unlikely that it will contain the same balanced mixture of health and growth promoting ingredients. Replace soil only back to the old level. Room must be left for watering. The new soil should be packed down tightly and watered in thoroughly.

Now for re-potting. Please do not think you are saving time by moving a plant from a little pot into a really big one. This does work outdoors where atmosphere and evaporation differ but indoors there is danger of the plant becoming bogged down by all the moist soil around it. The thing to do is to move the plant one size up each time. Thus a 60 will go on to a 48 and a 48 to a 32 and so on.

Earlier I mentioned John Innes compost, here perhaps a little clarification is called for. The John Innes Horticultural Institute, a famous research station, some years ago devised a formula for composts for pot plants—from the seedling to the final stage. It is based on sterilized soil which means that if this is used we do not have colonies of weeds growing up and competing with out pot plants for the right to occupy the pot. Into the soil go also ingredients to ensure correct drainage and balanced plant foods. This is not a proprietory preparation, the recipe may be found at the end of this chapter, but unless you have many plants it is unlikely to be economical to mix the compost yourself. Most garden shops, some florists and some department stores that have a garden section sell it. You can buy small quantities or several bushels. It is suitable for all plants of all kinds. I use it quite successfully for cacti. In fact I use nothing else.

In the bottom of the new pot (by the way if you are using a second-hand pot see that it is scrubbed clean and dried before you use it) you must place some drainage material. A few pieces of broken flower pot is the usual thing. This drainage ensures good aeration of the soil. Without this the drainage hole in the pot is likely to become plugged and the soil sodden.

While on the subject of aeration I should like to point out that this is much more important than many people realize. The reason why a plant will die in sodden soil is as much because the air spaces are filled with water and so the soil is unable to function properly as for any other. When we immerse a pot in a bucket of water so that its soil is covered we see a stream of air bubbles rise to the surface. As soon as the stream ceases and becomes the occasional bubble we should remove the plant or no air will remain at all.

Aeration of surface soil is important too and just as we fork over the garden border breaking up into smaller particles soil which has been beaten down by rain or baked by sun so should we carefully "fork" over the soil in the pots. This disturbance should not be allowed to go deep and so harm the roots. A stick or an old kitchen fork will do quite well. The fork supplied in some boxes of dates makes an excellent scratcher.

In a 60 pot one often finds that just a single crock, as broken flower pots are called, is placed over the drainage hole. A 48 pot will need three or four. Or if you are short of materials you can replace the crock removed from the root ball of the plant to be re-potted, place this over the hole and arrange a few stones or even very well washed clinker above it.

Over this drainage layer sift a little soil. Here you should take a little care for after re-potting it is important that the soil level of the plant is not changed. Therefore the amount of soil below it needs to be sufficient to bring it up to the same level in the new pot, no more and no less.

First inspect the root ball. If you have not already done so prise out the drainage cock (often the roots grow over this and hide it). And if the lower roots appear to have grown round and round or are tightly matted gently pull them apart at the base so that they are more likely to spread. If this is not done the roots will sometimes go on following their old course thus deriving no benefit from the new soil and larger root room.

Do not worry if when you do this some soil falls away. It is just as well if it does for it is almost sure to be spent and fairly worthless. Sweep it aside though, don't use it again or mix it in with the new compost.

The next thing we have to ensure is that the soil in the new pot is as dense as that in the old. If a difference is allowed to exist it is quite probable that the roots will not attempt to penetrate the loose soil as new and rich as it is. For this reason the new soil has to be rammed into position so that the two densities match.

Set the plant in position in the centre of the pot on a layer of soil which has been calculated to bring the potted plant up to the correct level. Now sift some new soil round the base of the root ball for a depth of say two inches. Use a spoon for this if you haven't a small trowel or even a chute of folded paper. As a rammer I use the handle of a wooden spoon from the kitchen. Ram the soil down with the end of this working evenly all round the old root ball. Stop ramming when you judge the two soil masses are about even in density. Add more soil and continue working this way until the final level is reached. Do not forget that there should be left, between the top soil level and the pot rim, a space for watering.

It is as well, right at the end of operations to hold the pot in two hands and give it a sharp tap, base on the table this time, just to settle the soil in among the roots.

If the plant is staked it is a good plan to leave the original stake in position. If the plant needs a new stake set it in position in the *fresh* soil where it can hurt no roots and where the new roots can find their way around it. Do this before ramming begins. Wait until re-potting is finished before taking out the old stake and re-tying the stems.

When all this is done we find that we run up against two schools of thought, one which says "don't water yet" and one which says "water right away".

Before saying more about this, just a word or two about the condition of any soil at potting time. Do not water the plant immediately before re-potting. It is important that the new soil and the old should be as alike in moisture content as possible. The potting compost should be neither damp nor dry. It should be crumbly and slightly moist to the touch rather like pastry mixture is before milk or water is added.

When I was taught to re-pot greenhouse plants the rule always was "no water at the roots only contsant spraying overhead". This was possible in a greenhouse of course. The idea was that if water was withheld from the pot soil the roots would go out in search of it. In the meantime overhead spraying and general humidity in the greenhouse prevented the plants from flagging unduly.

In the home conditions are quite different. For some time now I have made a practice of watering the plant immediately on re-potting. In this case though I throw away any water which has drained through the pot instead of leaving it to be taken up again. Sufficient water is given in the first place for the space between the top soil level and the pot to be filled.

If you have done your re-potting well the water should be sucked down fairly rapidly and you will have the satisfaction of knowing that it will take with it the soil and draw it in to all the crevices between the roots that are inaccessible to us.

After this do not be in a hurry to water the plant. Do not stand it in full sunshine for a few days (if it is the kind of plant that likes sun) and wait until the top soil is dry before attempting to give more water. After a few weeks and at a time you know the soil is not too dry, you may if curiosity drives you, turn the plant upside down as directed earlier and see if any new roots are appearing in the new soil. As a rule these are well covered with tiny root hairs. Sometimes almost fluffy in fact. This is an excellent sign. Your plant's digestion is good for it is through these tiny root hairs that the roots take in their plant foods in solution!

Well, what a lengthy lesson! But I make no apology for going into details of what is to a skilled gardener a simple business. I know from my postbag that these elementary things are those that worry a beginner. I know too that a plant given a good start is not likely to come to much harm.

If you wish to fill a bowl with plants the procedure is much the same except for one thing. As there is no outlet for the water one must guard against the possibility of any water which might lie in the bottom of the bowl becoming foul and smelly. We get over this in two ways. First a really good drainage layer is made, say as a general rule, a quarter the depth of the container—not more. This can be graduated so that there are a few large crocks on the floor, then smaller ones above them and smaller crushed crocks or bricks above this. If you have no crocks, use graduated stones but you can usually beg a broken pot from florist and ironmonger and crack this up for drainage.

Among this set some nuggets or pieces of charcoal to absorb any gases which might be given off by stagnant water. This charcoal can be bought from the chemist for a few pence. You need only a small quantity. An ounce goes a long way.

After these preparations arrange and plant the bowls.

Even if your knowledge of plants is not wide you will recognize the wisdom of placing plants of kindred tastes together should you wish to plant a mixed arrangement. Even in a plunged arrangement we have seen that it would be asking for trouble to place say a water-loving primula with a drought-loving sansevieria. By the same token, a bowl of ferns and primulas would not only look lovely but would be easy to tend.

Although I went into such detail about re-potting please do not imagine that all mixed plant arrangements must be planted, for the pots may be arranged in a container, some of them tilted to get a prettier effect and some raised a little so that we see them to advantage. However those that are tilted will have to be restored to their original position as soon as you find the stems curving upwards.

It is well worth while to have a collection of small pots, well filled with growth, that you draw upon for table decorations. If they are trailers such as tradescantia or hedera they may be tilted to cascade over the edge of a bowl. Pebbles, moss, Flora-pak or paper can be used to wedge them in position. Peat is good but likely to soil unless you make certain that no crumbs can fall off on to a clean cloth.

Plants may be tilted or even laid on their side to give the effect needed but they should not be left like this for long. After a few days the growing tips will start to grow in a different direction. As soon as this happens the plant should be restored to its proper position. It would probably go on growing this way but would defeat your purpose in doing so, if the purpose of laying it on its side was to hide the pot and give the impression that it was naturally trailing. The new direction of growth would reveal the pot. Furthermore plants are more trouble to water this way.

One of the daintiest kind of plant garden is a "pebble planter" —dainty because plants grown this way have a more delicate appearance than those grown normally. The leaves are smaller and often coloured differently. For example, a rooted *Philo-dendron scandens* some two years old has plum coloured tinted undersides to the foliage. All plants are slow growing.

Any kind of stones will do but if any have been gathered from the seashore they should be boiled or soaked and soaked until all the salt has been drawn away. Washed shingle is good. Transparent or opaque bowls or planters may be used. Fill them to within half an inch of the brim with pebbles and cover with water after adding a few pellets of charcoal.

Select the cuttings, arrange them among the pebbles which will weigh them down and so keep them in place. Hedera, plectranthus, zebrina, a chlorophytum runner, *Philodendron scandens*, creeping jenny and rhoicissus are growing in a planter seven inches across and two inches deep on a table in my room. Anything that will root in water will grow this way.

Little ferns should have the soil washed from their roots before being "planted".

Good Companions for Plant Communities

JOHN INNES COMPOSTS

J.I. Seed Compost

2 parts by loose bulk of medium loam
1 part by loose bulk of peat
1 part by loose bulk of sand

To each bushel of this mixture add:

$1\frac{1}{2}$ oz. superphosphate of lime
3/4 oz. finely ground chalk or limestone

J.I. Potting Compost

7 parts by loose bulk loam
3 parts peat
2 parts sand

To each bushel add 4 oz. of:

2 parts by weight hoof and horn meal
2 parts superphosphate of lime
1 part sulphate of potash
and finally add 3/4 oz. finely ground chalk or
limestone.

J.I. Cuttings Compost

1 part by loose bulk of medium loam
2 parts of peat
1 part of coarse sand
No fertilizer is added.

The loam used should always if possible be sterilized by steaming at 200 deg. F. for at least twenty minutes. It should not be too acid or too limy, but fairly neutral and should preferably be passed through a half-inch sieve. The sand should be very coarse and the peat free from dust.

CHAPTER SEVEN

IN SICKNESS AND IN HEALTH

I T SEEMS to me that unless one recognizes the differences in taste that exist between various plants one can never achieve success. At first the demands of certain plants can be a little bewildering and even more bewildering, to the beginner, can be technical advice intended to be helpful. For example a trained and knowledgeable gardener will talk glibly about a plant "being kept dry". Some plants leave the nursery with advice tags tied to them and on some of these will be written "keep dry in the winter". The non-technical gardener does just that and finds that his precious plant curls up and dies. How was she to know that what the nurseryman really meant was "keep comparatively dry in winter if your rooms are cold and not very light!"

In writing this book it has been brought home to me more than ever that the average indoor gardener, new to the craft, must most of the time be in utter confusion brought about mainly by technical jargon and by the blind handing down of certain advice which although good a hundred years ago can not be applied to the modern scene. Let me try to remedy that.

Even if you know little of botany or ecology your own observations will have shown you that some plants grow in bog, some in the lush moisture of meadow grass or hedgerow, some in the sand of the seaside and some in the crevices of the rocks. Some like to be baked hot and dry on the roof of a house and some like the cool dark shade of trees and grotto.

It so happens that in most cases it is impossible to coax a plant to change over. The bog plant will not live in dry sand nor the desert plant in a bog. The same maxim applies to plants grown under artificial conditions in pots. Because we know their origins it is possible to give them what they require. As I mentioned briefly in the previous chapter we can group them very roughly into succulents, semi-succulents, normal and water-loving. Of course some are most co-operative and will grow under most conditions.

I am afraid that it really is a case of getting to know them for yourself. There is a table at the end of the book and I think that this should be helpful.

The way a plant is watered influences it more than any other factor. Just think, it has been possible for the scientist to make up a recipe that suits all pot plants. True, many nurserymen still prefer to mix their own composts based on a particular plant's needs in its natural surroundings. But the interesting thing is that another nurseryman can use the scientist's mixture and turn out a plant which is just as good.

So we have bog loving plants like a cyperus or primula growing in the same mixture as the desert cactus or the jungle philodendron. But were we to give them all the same amount of water there would be a different story to tell.

First of all let us make quite sure that we all know what is meant by watering a plant. I have been so surprised at times to see a dessertspoonful of water carefully poured over a plant once a day or, at the other end of the scale, someone recently sought my advice because the leaves of a *Ficus decora* were falling. This gardener left the plant standing in a bowl with water halfway up the pot, all night once a week.

In previous chapters I have stressed several times that one should allow a free area between the top soil and the pot. This should be between a half-inch and an inch for a 60, and for a 48 more, because more water is needed for a larger plant. When the plant is watered this area should be filled. If the soil is well drained, and certainly if the soil is dry, the water will be quickly sucked through. This water should not be tipped away—you may think that it has been discarded because the soil is already wet enough—but this is not so, it should be left so that it can slowly be absorbed back into pot and soil. Actually if the pot soil is already moist or wet the water takes longer to drain through.

One question which is always being put to me is "How often should I water my plant?" I wish I could say every Monday or twice a week, but it is quite impossible to do so. So much depends on the plant's environment. It must be watered when it is thirsty. Some weeks it will dry out quicker than another. Some weeks the soil will remain damp for several days. However, it is quite easy, once you know how, to gauge whether the plant needs water or not.

There are several ways of doing this—some professional gardeners need only to look at a plant, but this is aiming high.

One good method is by sounding or tapping the pot, If it rings hollow, water is needed. If it rings dully then the soil is well charged. It takes a little practice to get the hang of it and then it is very simple indeed. By way of experiment take a pencil and with it tap an empty pot—you should get a real ring from this. Then rap a pot (if you have one) of a plant which should be kept on the dry side, say a cactus, peperomia, sansevieria or geranium. After that obviously you need to hear the contrasting sound so rap a pot that has just been watered or that you know to be damp. Use this method to test the pots when you have any doubts. It is infallible so long as you have a good ear.

Another method is testing the weight of the pot. But this is not always practicable especially where a plant is suspended or otherwise fixed in position.

I usually study the top of the pot soil. When the plant is ready for a drink a faint white crust appears over the surface. It disappears after water is added and reappears again when it needs re-charging.

So many successful indoor gardeners tell me "I water my plants once a week, every Saturday"—or something similar. There is no doubt that once you have worked out the personalities of certain plants this regular watering benefits plants, but not all of them. It certainly suits the long-standing and long-suffering philodendrons, ivies, rhoicissus and others of similar characteristics, but it would not suit the softer, quicker growing temporary plants such as primulas, azaleas, cyclamen, cinerarias and hydrangeas.

Some of these are greedy drinkers. I know I have often been surprised in the afternoon of a sunny day to see that these already need watering again even though they were watered that morning. That is why, where a plant will tolerate it, I like to let it "paddle". There is less danger then of it becoming flagged.

Should you find any plant flagging badly—first make sure that this is not due to over-watering and is merely the beginning of the end. Should it be dry immerse it in a bucket of water. See that the water comes just above soil level. It is not always a good thing (nor is it always harmful) to let the water be so deep that the foliage or flowers are immersed. The weight of the water will sometimes bruise them.

What you can do however to hasten the revival of a flagged plant is to roll the top leafy portion in newspaper. Immerse the pot and the water will travel slowly up the paper and so make a cool damp wall round the plant.

With some plants drying out is more dangerous than with others. Some like the berried solanums or heaths, once they have flagged can never be restored to their former glory. Leaves are shed, although blooms may be retained, and the plant looks very sorry for itself indeed.

During summer I give the permanent plant the luxury of a bath. The pot is immersed, and my goodness how rapidly the bubbles rise even though the plant has been watered regularly and shows no sign of lacking water. At the same time I wash the leaves. The plant is then taken out and left to drain. I usually use the bath for this purpose. Several thicknesses of newspaper at the side of the bath helps to drain the plant and keep the bath unscratched and reasonably clean.

Usually the first indication that something is wrong with a plant is the yellowing of the leaves. This precedes a fall although sometimes good green leaves will fall too. There are several reasons why this may happen. As I have already indicated, a rapid leaf fall is the result of the plant being allowed to become too dry at the roots. In this case the leaves will show some signs of dryness, usually round the edges.

When a plant appears to be perfectly healthy yet its leaves are falling, and when those same leaves are green and plump with no noticeable signs of any distress, the cause is almost certain to be over-watering. Sometimes, as with cyclamen, over-watering will also cause soggy yellow leaves.

If most of the leaves on a plant turn yellow fairly rapidly— I have seen geranium leaves turn yellow in two days—the cause is most probably poisoning by domestic gas. The geranium I referred to was set experimentally on my kitchen window-sill near which is a gas water heater. Although this has an out-let the small quantity of gas given off into the atmosphere was sufficient to kill the plant.

Where there is no gas present and the leaves are still yellow-ing it may be that the plant is not getting sufficient light but more likely it is suffering from suffocation. The surface of any leaf—and stems too—is covered with microscopic pores through which the plant breathes. Should these pores become clogged they cannot function. The leaf structure alters and be-ing useless to the plant is discarded. We see why it is so impor-tant that plants should be kept clean.

The green tissue in a leaf is due to the presence of chlorophyll which is made by certain cells in the leaf. These cells can work only in light. The amount of light needed varies according to the plant. The whole process is highly complicated but one simple fact remains—without light plants cannot live.

Another reason for leaf yellowing is the absence of a certain "food" in the soil. Some ferns, particularly the spiky *Asparagus sprengeri*, turn yellow when they are pot-bound. This is a plant that needs yearly re-potting. I once grew a whole greenhouse full of this fern planted in soil and I found that one had to be almost ruthless. All thin spindly shoots need to be cut away so that the vigorous growths have a better chance. I found too, that the soil was quickly starved. Pot grown it needs plenty of water, good feeding and constant change.

When I was a child I went to stay with my grandmother who although she lived in South-east London kept a goat. One day I noticed that he was behaving rather oddly, leaning against the fence and nodding his head drowsily. I went into the house and told my grandma. She came out to investigate and discovered that he had eaten all the leaves from her aspidistras and other house plants that she had stood in the yard to catch the summer rain. The other details of the incident I have forgotten. All I have remembered is that when a shower came in warm weather the plants were set outside so that their leaves might be cleansed and so that the good rain could course through the pot.

This is a good thing to do. Not all plants are suitable of course. I see no point in taking well-trained plants from a wall so that they may enjoy a shower. The problem of setting them back in the same position without damaging shoots or marking the wall is too great. But those plants which are easily moved do benefit, especially those with finely cut leaves which are difficult to clean. Among these are the ferns, some of which grow naturally where water drips or showers on them.

Plants with small leaves like the ivies are cleaned better by a good drenching shower than any other way. When cyclamen are to be started into growth again at the end of the summer it is a good plan to let a rain shower provide the first soaking.

The foliage of permanent plants become very dusty. The best way to clean a really dusty plant is to syringe it so that the dust is washed away without scratching.

Next to a syringe, a sponge is really the best material to wash the leaves although a cloth, tissue or cotton wool will do, of course. One should take care that in removing the dust the surface of the leaf does not become damaged. It might if you did this roughly. Use clean tepid water, try to wash the whole of one surface with one gentle stroke, squeeze out the sponge and wipe off surplus moisture.

A plant well looked after should gleam with health. Someone wrote to me in despair because a plant had died. She had looked after it so carefully, she told me, she had even sponged the leaves with olive oil to make them shine. Poor plant—suffocated to death! The oil clogged the pores and prevented them from doing their work.

Unless you are looking for a hobby that is time-absorbing it seems a pity to me to have to spend long hours on plant hygiene! I try to fit their care in with my daily round. Before dusting a room I check on plants and see what watering is necessary. This done, dusting the room begins and I make it a rule to dust three or four leaves on each plant each day as I do this. This way I find that the dust never gets thick enough to do any damage nor to become difficult to move. I find too that dusty, dying-to-have-a-wash plants don't pile up.

This has other advantages too. Daily handling of a plant means that pests do not get a chance to take a hold. On the occasion when we found that we had brought scale home we were soon able to eradicate it. It had attached itself under the leaves of the large ivy *Hedera ravenholst*. This plant was due to have a few leaves dusted and as I held one of the large lower leaves I felt a bump or pimple on the underside. On inspection I could see it was scale—a limpet-like insect that attaches itself to a plant and draws sustenance for itself from the tissues. It doesn't look like an insect for one is unlikely to see it move. Old-timers are brown and about ⅛th inch long and youngsters are paler.

My method of extermination is crude. I take a tissue, place it over the insect and squash it, wiping the portion of leaf quite clean. The prescribed method is to wipe or wash off the insects with a cloth soaked in soapy water or methylated spirit. A nicotine spray may be used if necessary.

We get few pests, indeed they really are not troublesome generally speaking. Plants come so clean from the nurseries that unless some insect finds its way into your house you have little to worry about.

Aphis, or greenfly (though all aphids are not green) which can fly might find their way to you even in a city. I discovered a very new colony just coming into existence under the leaf of a pilea; each insect was so tiny they were difficult to see. For these, and for most things we don't wish to have as tenants, we use an ordinary fly spray and we find this perfectly satisfactory. There is no point in going to the trouble and expense of getting in special insecticides when this will do.

CHAPTER EIGHT

BABIES ARE EASY

QUITE the most exciting part of growing plants is to be able to increase them. Technically this is known as plant propagation but to most of us it is magic. All you do is to pick a little shoot, or even just a leaf from a plant, place it in water and within a few days there is a root to be seen! In no time at all there are many roots and then the plant is ready to be potted on, ready to grow big enough to yield cuttings or leaves in its turn.

There are times when I get "cutting happy". I find a plant that seems to have plenty of shoots to spare and there am I pushing them into soil at the base of tall plants, poking them in among the stones of my dish garden to find out if this particular one will grow in water, searching out my vase cupboard for little glasses that will take a leaf or a shoot, until there are up and coming plants all over the place.

What fun it all is! There are some plants such as the tradescantias which are really best steadily replenished by striking cuttings. You can take these any time from spring till autumn. In fact they will root in winter too but they take much longer. It is better for the plant to let it grow away easily and quickly.

First of all let us make quite sure that we understand each other. I do not intend going into details of the propagation of all house plants. This really is a job for the skilled gardener with a heated propagating frame at his disposal. What I want to do is to suggest a few things that can be done easily, which will take only a few minutes, and which can be done in the home. I am assuming too, that this is a chapter for beginners.

The operation of picking off portions of a plant is known technically as "taking a cutting". The act of setting it in sand, soil, water or some other medium in which it can be induced to root is known as "striking a cutting". Cuttings vary considerably, a shoot from the growing tip of a plant, a section of stem, a portion of root, a snip of leaf, or a leaf can all act as cuttings.

The tips of some plants, such as tradescantia, plectranthus, rhoicissus, philodendron, impatiens and hedera, are among the easiest of all. As a rule the shoot is cut or nipped out about a quarter-inch below a leaf. The lower leaf or leaves are trimmed off in case they lie in soil or water and so create a source of infection. This bare portion of stem is then inserted into whatever rooting medium is chosen.

If you're in a hurry, or if your fingers aren't really very green, you can use one of the several synthetic hormone powders to hasten and ensure the rooting of your cutting. These hormones are rather interesting and perhaps we can just take a quick glance at them here.

We all know that certain hormones in our own bodies play a vital part in our well being. And it's just the same with plants. Some of these organic chemicals play vital parts in certain aspects of growth and development and we can make use of them in indoor as well as outdoor gardening. Hormones can be used to promote the formation of roots, the subject we are on at the moment. But others can promote fruit formation, delay fruit dropping, retard growth or even kill weeds.

Many of these hormones can be produced synthetically and this is what we get in these proprietory brands. We can use the root-promoting hormones either in powder or liquid form. When a cutting has been taken from the parent plant, it can either be dipped into a hormone powder or placed in about a quarter of the dilute solution. In the latter case the cuttings should be left for twelve hours or so, then removed, washed in clean water and planted in the usual way.

These hormones are not things to fool around with. They should be used exactly as prescribed on the labels or instructions of the makers, for delicate variations in strengths of solutions (sometimes even two parts in a million) are advised for different types of plants.

If you are interested, some of the synthetic hormones are composed of alpha-naphthalene-acetic acid, indolyl-butyric acid, beta-indolyl-acetic acid and naphthoxyacetic acid. So now you know. But don't worry about them. I never use any of them for indoor plants.

Those plants I have just mentioned can be rooted in plain water. All you do is this. First find some small glass containers to hold the water. Tablet bottles or mustard jars will do. I like them to be decorative while they are about the place so I prefer to use dainty little glass vases which I collect for the purpose. The "rose" vase designed to take one flower is ideal.

You can if you wish place more than one cutting in a glass. To hold them in position cut a ring of paper a little wider than the mouth of the glass. Secure it in position with a rubber band or a little transparent tape and with a pencil or knitting needle make holes round the paper to take the cuttings. All the plants that root in water will also root in clean, moist sand. You really need silver or agricultural sand for this purpose—you can get as little as threepennyworth from an ironmonger—because builders' or sea-shore sand is likely to contain ingredients injurious to the plant.

These plants will also root in the pot compost but sometimes not quite so quickly. They appreciate more a mixture of half sand and half compost with the sand as a top layer. The plants can be potted on to compost. A mixture of half sand, half powdered peat, may also be used successfully.

You can plant several cuttings to a pot, round near the rim

in a ring, if you wish to save space. When they are rooted, tip out the root ball very gently and divide them into separate plants.

Prepare the pot or seed pan into which the cuttings are to be struck. (Incidentally they will root easier in a firm compost than in a loose one, so ram it down a little—don't overdo this though or watering becomes difficult.) Next make a little hole to take the stem. I use a pencil. Try to gauge the depth so that the stem just fits in. Insert the stem and then push the pencil down at an angle at the side so that the cutting is firm and the hole in which it is set filled in at the same time. Give the pot a sharp tap and water the cuttings to settle them in.

The rooting medium should be damp and it should not be allowed to dry out. To prevent excessive evaporation one can place a jam-jar, a transparent food cover or even a plastic bag over the pot. It might be possible to leave these covers on until the cutting roots. If however there seems to be an excessive amount of moisture forming on the inside remove the jar and wipe it dry. A plastic bag needs only to be turned inside out and the dry side in then inside. Should you see mildew on any leaves remove them and give a little more ventilation by taking the cover off for ten to fifteen minutes each day.

Cuttings taken this way may be more satisfactory but they are not so much fun because it is impossible to watch the daily progress of the roots. One must gauge when they are ready for potting either by gently tugging at them or by tipping out the entire contents of the pot—say any time after two weeks.

To me a leaf cutting is always an endless source of interest. It seems a miracle that one can push a *Begonia rex* leaf in a little vase of water and after some days roots emerge from the base and then one day a little cluster of miniature leaves appear too—a new plant has been born right before our eyes.

Not all plants can be propagated this way. But the begonias, peperomia, saintpaulia, gloxinia are easy to do. I remember seeing row on row of leaf cuttings of ficus, saintpaulia and chunks of sansevieria each standing up like a little flag when I visited one famous nursery. But here, of course, temperature and humidity were different from what you would find at home.

I find that it is important to take a mature, though not a fading, leaf rather than a young specimen. The older leaf takes water better. Cut the leaves with about two inches of stem. Set each in a jar of water. If there is difficulty in making them stay in place cut out a ring of fine card and make a hole through which to pass the stem. The card will lie on the top of the jar, support the leaf blade and prevent rapid evaporation. The new leaves will form at the base of the leaf-stalk or petiole.

All the rex begonias are good but I have been particularly successful with the variety called stellata. This has star shaped leaves which are extremely handsome. The leaves root very quickly in water and in no time at all, or so it seems, the tiny leaves are forming in a dense cluster.

There is another method of taking begonia cuttings which is quite fascinating and which you might like to try for the fun of it. The leaf is laid face downwards on a table or bench and the veins are cut with a sharp knife. The veins spread out from the stalk and then divide. They travel towards the margin of the leaf and then divide again. One must make the cuts, from a half to an inch according to the thickness of the vein, just below the division, that is, on the side nearest the stem.

Have ready a 50–50 mixture of peat and sand in a box or seed pan. See that it is moist.

An inch or so of stem should have been left on the leaf. Holding the cut leaf carefully on the palm of your hand, turn it the right way up. Make a hole for the stem in the compost and lay the leaf flat. The buried stem will help to hold it in place. See that all the surface of the leaf is quite flat. Plantlets should spring from the cut areas. Cover the box or pan with glass or transparent plastic. When the plantlets are well formed pot them up.

Speaking of plantlets—many plants, including some ferns, form plantlets on leaves or fronds. These may be potted.

Once cuttings form plants they ought to be moved into soil compost otherwise they will starve and die. Do not use a very large pot for this first move, much better to re-pot the young plant as soon as the roots begin to "go round the pot". You can tell if the plant is ready by knocking it out and if you can see a root or two on the outside of the soil then it is time to move it on to a larger pot. Do not wait for the plant to become root bound. A young plant like this needs, as gardeners say, to be kept moving.

Before we discuss re-potting it would be better to describe how the cutting is treated once it has made roots. If it is to be pot grown, see that plenty of drainage is provided. Sift a little soil over this. Gently remove the cuttings. Once out of water the roots are apt to cling together, but you should try to get them to spread out over the soil. Hold the cuttings in place with one hand while you gently sift in the soil with the other, so that it goes between the roots and so gently pushes them apart, as well as going over them. At the end give the pot a sharp tap and the plant a drink in the same way that you would if you were re-potting.

Some plants increase themselves vegetatively, in much the same way as a strawberry does when it sends out runners, tiny plants on the end of a long stem, a stolon, attached to the parent plant, whence it receives sustenance until its roots are formed and it can fend for itself.

One of the most enchanting of this type of plant is the *Saxifraga sarmentosa*. To see it at its best it needs to be suspended—in a window is a good place for it likes the sun. It should be fed and watered regularly. At first the stolons appear very neatly as little rosettes encircling the mother plant, but gradually they grow longer and longer, streaming down from the plant like ribbons from a posy. Each of the tiny rosettes will make a new plant should you wish. The best method really is to fill a little pot with moist soil and let the tiny plant rest on the surface. With your finger push the runner into the soil a little way to anchor the plant or hairpin it in position. When the roots have grown (you can judge this by gently trying to pull the plant out) sever it from the runner. *Saxifraga sarmentosa*, like the tradescantias and zebrinas is best renewed constantly as the old plants soon tire and look shabby.

Chlorophytum may be propagated in the same manner.

If you find taking "water" cuttings entertaining consider making a little colony of them and watch them grow together. You need a large narrow-necked jar for this; a goldfish bowl is good, or you can buy a dark green jar specially designed, which can be hung on the wall. This has a perforated tray which fits in the throat. The cuttings are pushed down through the holes into the water. The tray holds them in place. A foil tray, easily cut, can be used in the same manner.

The cuttings may be as mixed as one wishes. I have had plectranthus, tradescantias, ivy and philodendron growing together. Once the roots are well formed some plant food should be given. This needs to be in small doses as the tablets dissolve quickly in water. Say a quarter or a half tablet at a time. Once a fortnight might be sufficient, but one has to use discretion. If the plants (as they are now that they have roots) seem slow to grow, give the food a little more often.

Obviously cuttings are best taken from vigorous, healthy plants. Not only does this ensure that the children plants stand every chance but also that the plant itself does not suffer from being robbed. However, there is no doubt that it benefits a plant to prune it.

If you have any trailer (philodendron is an obvious example) that sends out long shoots a large portion of which are green but leafless, you would be well advised to cut it right back to the first good leaf. This seems ruthless, but it is no more so than the hard pruning of the roses in the garden. If you can bring yourself to do it—and I know the decision is a hard one to take—you will find yourself well rewarded. The best time for this pruning is the end of March.

I can offer you some little compensation until the plant springs anew. Use the growing tips of the trails that have been cut away as cuttings and split the difference by starting a new plant into life.

Occasionally one hears of a *Ficus decora* losing its lower leaves because of some lack of care (as I have described earlier). Will fresh leaves grow again, I am asked, or what can I do to improve the appearance of my plant. Once again the remedy calls for ruthlessness.

The leaves will not grow again on the lower trunk if the plant is left as it is. But as every true leaf bears a bud, that is, a potential shoot in its axil, we can do something to coax these sleeping shoots into growth. The top of the plant must be cut off, leaving a few leaves, one or two if the fall has been very drastic, on the old stem.

The severed top is not useless. It is in fact a fine cutting. Prepare a pot for it, a 48 is better than a 60 even though the plant should appear small, simply because in a small pot it is inclined to be top heavy. Make a mixture of 50 per cent sand and 50 per cent potting compost.

In the meantime nurse the remains. The more leaves that remain on this the better will it prosper, for a plant must rely on leaves as well as roots for its food supply.

If the original leaf fall was caused by over-watering (and this is the most frequent cause), see that the soil gets a chance to dry out. When possible spray the plant or swish it over with a clean brush dipped in water. So that the soil does not become soaked again, lay a folded newspaper over the top of the pot to catch the drips.

Watch the plant carefully for signs of activity. When one

bud or more begins to swell give it a plant tablet, plant food or liquid manure—rather as you would give a tonic to a convalescent. If and when the plant does grow it will not follow its original single stemmed form but is more likely to branch out into two or three stems.

If a ficus becomes too tall the same procedure can be taken. Cut out the growing tip so that the plant is induced to "break".

The division of certain plants is not difficult and appeals to the tidy-minded gardener who instead of having an untidily massed plant can view with pride a row of two, three or even four "new" plants. It is usually quite easy to tell when a plant needs dividing. Instead of the individual plant rising up fairly simply from soil level, one now sees a mass of growth which sometimes appears to be several plants jostling each other. When the roots are inspected they are almost sure to be matted.

Have pots and soil ready—cater for a few more than you need for often a plant needs division more than one realizes and the new portions come away readily and are more numerous than one expected. Tip the plant out on a sheet of paper so that you can clear up easily afterwards and gently shake away the drainage crocks, if they persist, and the loose soil from the roots. Handle these gently and gradually disentangle them pulling the plant apart. The portions will be quite distinct. They may in some cases have to be snapped off from the main root but when they are isolated there should be no doubt that they are a distinct plant.

Speaking generally I should not meddle with my plants merely for the sake of doing so, but with some plants it is quite obvious that they are bursting their bounds and that not even a move into a larger pot will really benefit them. Primulas, some ferns, chlorophytum, impatiens and aspidistra are examples.

Sometimes the roots are so massed, and this is particularly the case with ferns, that one can do no more than to cut the root mass into chunks, each with a top knot of green. First slice off

Left: Plants should not be hung too high in a room for they dry out quickly in the warm upper layers of air.

Below: On the left is a terra cotta "pocket" pot made on the same principle as a strawberry barrel. Each pocket holds a different kind of plant. In the centre is *Chlorophytum capense.* *Ficus decora's* pot is inside the ornamental pot which matches that of the ivy above. The pocket pot is turned daily so that the plants have equal share of the light. An upright growing plant is best seated in the centre of a group.

 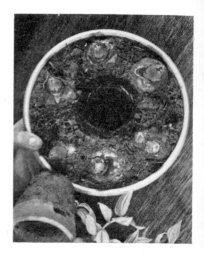

To make a pretty bowl garden, when bulbs are planted in fibre or soil, set them in a ring not quite touching each other round the bowl. In the centre place an empty three inch pot. Leave this in the bowl while the bulbs are rooting in a cool dark place. When they are brought into the light, remove the pot and replace it with a plant. This may be knocked from its pot. (It may then be smaller than the hole.) Any space between it and the bulb should be filled in, or the entire pot and plant may be planted. Ivies, tradescantia and *Peperomia glabella* are good evergreens, or small flowering plants such as primulas azaleas or ferns may be used as more permanent residents.

the base, drainage and all. After dividing plants treat them a little tenderly. Avoid giving them too much water. Spray overhead instead if this is practicable and keep them out of the sun.

Quite often successful gardeners find that their plants grow too well; they become much too tall. One way of remedying this is to pinch out the growing tip and so induce the plant to branch out. Early in this chapter I told how it is possible to root the tip of a ficus as a cutting, but there is no need where the plant is healthy to sever the cutting from its parent until it has rooted!

The usual methods of taking and striking cuttings is age-old. Recently, owing to the introduction of transparent plastic more than anything else, a new method has been invented, applied and found to be most effective. This is known as air-layering. For the home grower I imagine that this operation is particularly fascinating and entertaining. The plant is encouraged to produce roots by first cutting upwards a deep notch, one third the depth of the stem. Some experts recommend wedging open this cut with a match. Over this and right round the stem is laid a wad of damp sphagnum moss. This should cover at least three inches of the stem. It needs to be bound firmly with raffia. To prevent evaporation the moss should be covered with transparent plastic. The roots take something like two months to grow into the moss ball. The new plant is then cut from the old below the moss which should be left on and potted.

Ficus needs to be taken from about a foot from the growing tip and one may then expect the lower portion of the plant to branch out.

Air-layering is a means of tidying up some plants. As dieffenbachia and dracaena grow older the tuft of leaves are borne higher and higher on the tip of a trunk. This is not attractive, so unless there is a special reason for keeping a tall plant it is best to air-layer the plant at the top of this trunk making the notch below the lowest leaf.

CHAPTER NINE

THE END IS ALSO THE BEGINNING

THE vogue for house plants is a comparatively new one, developing since the war in a big way as I have already mentioned. It appeared to begin in Scandinavia, was taken up by the United States and parts of Europe and gradually grew in this country. Professional nurserymen here looked on it at first as a craze or fashion which would soon pass and only one or two of them made up their minds at once that this was something bigger. In the past ten years or so there have been many predictions that the phase would soon pass, but specialist nurserymen report larger and larger sales.

One reason for this is that the trade is not static. New plants are constantly being introduced and old and familiar subjects gradually dropped. The new varieties and the new plants practically without exception are grown and are accepted by the public because they are attractive in appearance and because they are easy to grow. Many of the old familiars have been replaced by new varieites which are easier to grow, last better, have a more appealing appearance or habit of growth. Ten years ago, for example, the ivies *Hedera helix Chicago, H. h. Pittsburgh* and *H. canariensis* were more or less the limit of this family available to the public. Today these are still to be seen, but in smaller quantities. Their places have been taken by a host of "new" ivies, recognizable as such but different in form, colour and habit of growth.

There is much greater colour available and house plants are rapidly losing their alternative label of green plants. Some foliage colour is now brilliant in the extreme. The fierce scarlets of some of the bromeliads, the new white, yellow and red long-lasting blooms on many plants, the metallic silvers and purples of *Begonia rex* and the bright variegations on many leaves are all examples of the greater emphasis on colour.

Not long ago one nurseryman sent an investigating team overseas. This team, all experts, went to the famous producers of house plants in several countries and to every other producer they could discover. They were not satisfied merely to look at lists or examine plants in show glasshouses. They scoured each nursery, looking in corners, under the shelving, peering and prying. They were not seeking to uncover secrets, merely to discover the odd forgotten plant, the failed experiment or the freak. They came back with more than 200 "new" house plants.

Some of these will never appear in commerce, either because they are too delicate for popular care, or because they are too difficult to rear or because they take too long to propagate. But all are now the subject of intensive experimentation. Even if they pass their tests and are shown to be suitable for the brutal maltreatment they may receive at the hands of sometimes unthinking buyers there is still much to do. They cannot be put on the market until a very considerable reservoir of plants has been collected. This may take years. At the same time other plants, hundreds of thousands of them, must patiently be grown, cuttings must constantly be taken, young plants must be repotted and grown on and hardened off ready for the market.

It is a wonder sometimes that we get any new plants at all. Many new plants are such subtle variations on the familiar that they are recognized as new only by the experts. For example the familiar India Rubber plant, *Ficus elastica* is seen all over the country, yet how many know that it has undergone a change for the better, that the *Ficus elastica* is comparatively seldom seen today and that what is recognized as such is really *Ficus elastica decora*, with leaves held more upright, a more sturdy plant altogether.

The humble tradescantia, known, used and popular long before the house plant vogue, has, like Bottom, been translated. On a special shelf in my London home I now have eight plants. All belong to the tradescantia family. All are different. All are attractive and easy to grow.

For some years now we have had the yellow and green striped, or golden, and the white and amethyst silver tradescantias. There is also the thicker leaved purple backed zebrina a near relation. Actually the tradescantia, or spiderworts, are grown in many gardens without their owners being aware that they belong to the same family as the pretty little indoor trailers, for these garden plants are apt to be untidy, with long swordlike leaves which criss-cross each other around a central purple flower.

If your indoor tradescantia blooms, you can see the family likeness and with some of the new kinds it is also possible to recognize them if you see them together. But some are mighty handsome!

Quadricolour has the brightest amethyst undersides, while the surface of the plant is light and dark green and grey, the pales pink and rosy purple. Imagine it!

Tradescantia regina has deep violet backs to long pointed leaves. These are green and grey-green banded with purple zones around the midrib. Blosfeldiana is thick and chunky with plain green slightly hairy leaves, but once again with coloured undersides a soft purple with much silver down.

Purpurea is a slightly smaller version with more colour on the top surface. There are others to come I understand and I can see that the tradescantia is going to be lifted out of its humble though popular position and placed on a pedestal (literally) in many homes.

By no means new, but comparatively seldom seen in the average home is the flamingo plant, or tail flower, *Anthurium scherzerianum*. It gets its name from the striking coral pink or red of its flower or from the little curly pig's tail spadix which protrudes from the glossy spathe which forms the bloom. Anthuriums are Aroids, members of the arum family. For many years they have been listed as stove plants and only comparatively recently has it been recognized that they are much more hardy than originally thought. I have heard of one plant which has been growing in a Dutch sitting-room for ten years and is still going strong!

The anthurium may be grown in the same way as hyacinth, in a glass, wedged in place and its crown lifted from the water level by a wisp of Osmuda fibre or a piece of cardboard. Whether in water or soil, the plant should be kept out of full sunshine and hot, dry, draughts. It likes plenty of light but cannot stand too cool an atmosphere. Frost will kill it immediately.

Another quite new plant which created a minor sensation when it appeared massed for the first time at Chelsea Flower Show is *Aphelandra squarrosa louisae*. This is a green plant with long leaves strikingly striped with pale gold. It is usually surmounted with a large cockscomb flower, yellow in colour. Since the aphelandra was first introduced it has proved somewhat disappointing, as few owners have been able to keep it for long periods. I found this to be so myself and I have discussed it with Mr. Tom Rochford who introduced it to this country. After some experiments on both sides we have agreed to classify it as a "temporary" plant in the same way that one might so call a cyclamen or azalea. It will live for weeks, even months, in the home, but to keep it for years is a more difficult proposition.

Mr Rochford did, however, send me some most helpful notes about the aphelandra and from them I have culled the following information. The main part of the aphelandra head is really a series of bracts from which emerge, pair by pair, yellow flowers shaped somewhat like a shrimp. These fall out in due course as new pairs keep on coming until they reach the top of the yellow bract. This bract remains yellow for some time after the flowers have all fallen and then slowly turns green. Eventually the bract itself will fall off. It is best to cut it back before this happens. Do not just remove the bract itself but cut it back to a good pair of leaves. This will encourage side shoots to grow from leaf joints and these in time will grow strong and produce more bracts and flowers.

Nurse the plant carefully through the winter but see that the soil is always moist, not wet and never let it get really dry. If it gets too dry the plant will flag. The leaves will hang down and may fall off. Be careful not to damage the leaves. If they are torn or slit down brown patches will start up around the damage and will spread over the leaf. Once a leaf is damaged like this nothing can be done except to remove the whole leaf.

During late autumn and especially through the winter months always water an aphelandra with tepid water. It does not like shocks from icy water. It likes to be in as warm a position as possible in the home, 50-60 deg. F. is ideal, but do not stand it very near an open fire or radiator. It will stand a drop of temperature down to 42 deg. F. but not for long periods.

Keep the plant out of sunlight. It likes semi-shade. It also likes humidity. This can be achieved in the home by standing the plant on a tray filled with coarse shingle or pebbles containing some water. Never allow the bottom of the plant to stand in the water. So says Mr. Rochford, and you can take what he says as gospel. Good luck to you with your aphelandras, for they are among the most charming and colourful of house plants and it would be a great pity if they did not receive full acceptance simply because they are a little difficult.

It is very noticeable that a large proportion of these "new" plants are colourful. They produce colours other than green. The philodendron, for example, was one of the first of the house plants to catch the public imagination after the war. The popular *Philodendron scandens* was for a time to be seen prominently in the foreground of every picture in the fashionable home magazines. This was due not only to its decorative qualities but also to the fact that it is tolerant of home living conditions. But the picture is beginning to change. More and more philodendrons with more and more colour are appearing on the scene, some of them having quite different characteristics and making different demands upon us.

Philodendrons belong to the family Araceae. They are nearly all climbers, with aerial roots which may or may not actually be utilized. Leaf shapes vary from the regular heart-shape of the old scandens to the notched, indented, lobed and cut leaves of some of the less common plants.

Two of the new philodendrons are *P. melanochrysum* (from the Greek *melas*, "black") with a beautiful near-black velvet leaf surface, and *P. ilsemanii*, with a finely marbled and mottled cream and green colouring. Both these are climbers. They will grow up a mossed cane and the aerial roots as they develop may either be ignored or potted up at various levels.

The new philodendrons are perhaps a little less easy to manage than the old. They like some degree of warmth and humidity. Neither enjoy full sunlight but both must have good light to enable them to retain their leaf colouring.

The shiny leaved varieties are easy enough to keep clean, for the foliage can be sprayed and swabbed. But velvety or hairy leaves are more difficult. If they get too damp they burn or curl when drying out and of course dust cannot be swabbed from their surface. So blow the dust off. If your lungs aren't up to the task, I know someone who unashamedly and unconcernedly uses a pair of fire bellows!

Do not allow the new philodendrons to become dry. Keep out of draughts and in a fairly warm place where the temperature fluctuates as little as possible. They should get good light without direct sunlight. They grow quickly, so after having a plant for a year or so keep watch on the root system.

To describe another comparatively new plant and one which is striking and appealing in appearance, may I ask your mind to be filled with a mental picture of a *Begonia rex*, that wonderful foliage plant with its purple and silver, its metallic sheen. Now extend your imagination to see the same plant but with somewhat smaller leaves. Finally look upwards and see this plant growing, climbing in true vine form. You have been imagining a *Cissus discolor*.

The same colours, the same metallic sheen, with red-purple under-leaves and coral pink stems. Wonderful, of course, but the *Cissus discolor* has its drawbacks. In the first place it is semi-deciduous, losing some of its leaves in the autumn. Secondly, it is a real heat lover. It calls for higher temperatures indoors during the winter than we can normally guarantee in this country—temperatures in the 75 to 85 deg. F. bracket.

If you feel that you can grow it (and really, even if you can't keep it permanently it is well worth growing as a temporary plant) then give it plenty of light and plenty of warmth. It likes to stay in one position and when treated well will respond with rapid growth. Don't let it get cold or sit in a draught.

Now we run into a spot of name trouble. There is another plant with a roughly similar name, a roughly similar appearance and a roughly similar habit which I must also recommend. It is the *Dioscorea discolor*. The dioscorea is, surprisingly, a hardy tuberous rooted climbing perennial. More surprisingly, still, it is a member of the "Yam" family and the large milky tuber may be cooked and eaten like a potato as, in fact, has been done for centuries in the tropical south seas and Far East.

Heart shaped leaves, the growing habit of the vine and its deciduous nature make it similar in so many respects to the *Cissus discolor*, but the main difference is in the leaf surface. The cissus has a shiny surface and the dioscorea a velvety texture.

The deciduous nature of the plant means that its sale is limited to the warmer months of the year. It can, actually, be grown out of doors. It demands no special soils nor any great degree either of heat or humidity. It likes the sun. In September it begins to shed its leaves and in October the tubers are apt to come to the surface of the pot. They should be lifted and stored in a frost proof place. In the early spring they should be planted again two or three inches deep and watering should begin and be increased as the plant grows more vigorously.

Do not over-water or over-heat. Do not attempt to stimulate the plant to growth during its resting period. If the tuber is left in its pot over winter, do not give any water until early spring, then water sparingly at first and give a slight degree of warmth.

In the past year or two there has been a considerable development in the use of orchids as house plants. If they are carefully chosen and grown with just a little extra attention they do quite well and of course some of the blooms that one can obtain are simply wonderful and they last for ages.

There is, unfortunately, a little snobbery in the orchid world and consequently these plants have had the exotic label tagged to them. They are thought to be both expensive and difficult. Many are. But one or two firms have prepared special lists of plants that can be grown quite well indoors needing only a little more humidity than is necessary for other house plants.

One nurseryman has produced a special list of orchids for indoors. He has divided the plants listed into those that will grow in a north window and those that will grow best with a southern aspect. The former do well in temperatures between 45 and 60 deg. F., quite a moderate living-room range, while the second group like to be just a little warmer, between 45 and 75 deg. F. The main thing is to give these plants a little extra moisture in the air and this is done by standing their pots on trays of shingle or vermiculite which are kept moist. The water dries out and sends waves of humid air upward around the plants. Collections of four plants plus a tray of shingle cost only five or six pounds.

One good way to grow orchids indoors is to have a glass case made which can stand right in the window. If it is built on the principle of a Wardian case, surrounded completely with glass and more or less airtight, then the plants automatically get the humidity they require. But this is a bit much for most of us. We can't spare the space in our windows.

Using the simple tray method we should be able to get quite good results if the plants are chosen carefully. But remember that orchids must have light. The tray should be placed in a window with the front edge about a foot from the glass except in very bright sunshine, when it should be pulled back another foot into the room. The tray should contain an inch or so of water, preferably rain water. This will help evaporation and yet give adequate drainage to the plants. Make sure there are no draughts. The windows can be opened in the summer months, but only so that no wind comes whistling in right on to the plants.

As with so many other plants, orchids should never be given too much water. If in doubt, leave out. Let the plants dry out almost completely before watering them again. Only very seldom and in the driest of conditions should room orchids be watered more than once or so a week.

Spraying is helpful. A light spray with clean water (again preferably rain water) is helpful and the leaves should be given a wipe every now and again to keep them clean. Water should be at room temperature to avoid any unnecessary shock to the root system.

If you get any pests on your orchids an occasional spray with a DDT solution will get rid of them. Under normal conditions this shouldn't really be necessary. Re-potting is another thing that is hardly necessary. Most plants come in soil and in a size pot that will enable them to live quite happily for a couple of years. Orchids don't like too large a pot and will never flower so well if they feel a bit lost in a home too large for them.

The End is Also the Beginning

What orchids can you grow indoors ? Well, in a cool room you can grow several of the *Cypripedium insigne* hybrids such as Sanderae. These are some of the familiar "slipper" orchids. Or you can enjoy the large crimson flowers of *Masdevallia harryana*, the wonderful showers of small yellow flowers freely produced from the *Oncidium spacelatum*, or the "scorpion orchids" long sprays of brilliant orange-red flowers. The *Vanda coerulea* will give you flowers of a wonderful and unusual blue. There are many more.

Among the group that like it just a little warmer you have even a wider choice. Just imagine these, for example: *Cymbidium tracyanum*, with sweetly scented spikes of large orange-brown flowers; *Dendrobium nobile*, white and amethyst flowers; *Laelia autumnalis*, with four or five bright purple blooms; *Odontoglossum grande*, five to seven yellow-brown flowers on a spray; *Epidendrum o'brienianum*, brilliant red flowers in clusters which open one at a time. Well worth the money for that something a little different, aren't they ?

In addition to the "new" plants that have come our way in the past few years, there are also new techniques which are well worth mentioning. Both in the commercial and the amateur horticultural scene, the advantages of polythene sheeting have been discovered and exploited. Polythene sheeting is now widely used among commercial growers to line their glass-houses. This has been found considerably to raise inside temperatures, which of course leads to great economies in the use of fuel for heating them. This in itself may not be of great interest to the person who grows house plants in the home, but it gives a hint. For example, windows can have polythene sheeting pinned over them. This allows in plenty of light yet makes the room warmer and obviates the danger of draughts. This is not practical for a room that is being used normally, but from what I have heard a spare room or box room is frequently used as a plant nursery and here this method can profitably be employed.

The material may also be used to construct simply and cheaply a small propagating house. It has several advantages over glass, being lighter in weight, considerably less expensive and much easier to work with.

Another use for polythene which I have tried myself with excellent results is to use the normal polythene bags so often brought home from the greengrocer, as seed boxes. They are particularly useful for forcing seeds into early growth. I place a trowel full of good soil into the polythene bag, making sure that it is moist but not wet. The seeds are planted in this in the normal way, the top of the bag taken up and tied so that the bag is more or less airtight. I then place it in an airing cupboard for gentle heat. In almost no time the seeds have germinated. The warm moist atmosphere inside the bag is just as it would be in any propagating house. After the seeds have begun to get away, the top should be opened to give the new plants some air and they should be removed from the airing cupboard to some other warm light place in the house. The seeds will continue to grow safely enough in the bags, which may be treated as any seed box.

I have propagated a number of seeds in this way in January, thus giving the young plants a good early start in life. Obviously this is a highly artificial and frankly rather risky way of going about things and there has been a proportion of failures. Several young plants have been unable to stand the pace and have just curled up and expired. But I have had just as good results by using the more conventional forcing methods under glass in a heated greenhouse as speed of germination is greater.

Still another use of polythene is in the lining of an otherwise unlined or leaky container. This is so obvious that it is with real chagrin that I must report that I learned the method from a friend Bob Boulter, a Sussex nurseryman. He makes his own troughs from waste timber, still covered with bark. Very attractive they are, but not waterproof. This means that when they have been watered they leak and this will obviously not do when they are to be used for indoors. So he lined the interiors of these boxes or troughs with a simple polythene bag. This lasts indefinitely, is completely inconspicuous and costs only a penny or two against the shillings or more it would cost to have tin linings made. I have one of his troughs at present in my office, planted up with a number of ivies and other attractive plants. It still looks well after many months and not once has a drop of water leaked on to the table where it stands.

Another method of house plant culture for the home, which is becoming increasingly popular, makes use of the hydroponic system of growth. No soil is used. The plants grow entirely in a liquid solution of plant foods; salts and minerals.

The plants themselves are held in a small container not unlike a small flower pot, even to a hole in the bottom, which is, actually, rather larger than the conventional one. This is filled with gravel or granite chips to hold the roots in place. This pot drops into another, larger container which holds the solution. This liquid is simplicity itself, for it is merely tap water plus a special plant tablet dissolved in it. Once a month or so the liquid is thrown away and replaced by fresh water and a fresh tablet.

The roots grow through the gravel, down through the hole in the root pot and into the solution. The solution has been built up chemically to give all the necessary food to the plant. I haven't tried this method myself but I have seen plants growing this way and very good they looked too. I would not say that there is any specific advantage in this means of plant culture, but I do say that it is a new idea, that it saves messing about with soils and pots, and of course it does away completely with the constant and ever present risk of over-watering.

PLANT TREATMENT
CHART

NAME	DESCRIPTION	LIKES	DISLIKES	WATER	FEED
Abutilon	Flowering shrub.	Warm conditions summer and winter. Sun. Pruning in spring.	Cold, dry heat. Too much water in winter.	Freely in summer, carefully in winter.	Freely in summer, not in winter.
Adiantum	Maidenhair fern.	Warmth, humidity.	Cold, draughts, smoke, gas, direct sun or heat.	Freely, always while warm.	Sparingly.
Aechmea	Pineapple family. Large, fleshy leaf rosettes, sometimes richly coloured.	Warmth, humidity overhead spraying, light.	Cold, dry air. Over-watering.	Moderately. Carefully in winter.	Sparingly.
African Violet (see Saintpaulia)					
Agapanthus	African lily. Blue flowered bulb plant.	Well drained pot, moist conditions. Sun.	Dry soil, dry air.	Freely in summer, carefully in winter.	Freely in summer.
Agave	Succulent, with leaf rosettes.	Sunlight. Dry conditions.	Damp conditions. Cold, draughts.	Moderately in winter, seldom in summer.	Sparingly.
Aichryson	Succulent. Formerly Sempervivum.	Warm, sunny conditions.	Cold, draughts, over-watering.	Moderately in summer, rarely in winter.	Never.

144

	Description	Likes	Dislikes	Watering	
Aloe	Succulent with thick prickly leaves.	Well drained pot, warmth, light.	Cold, damp conditions.	Moderately in summer, rarely in winter.	Seldom, in summer only.
Ananas	Pineapple.	Warmth, sun, humidity.	Cold, dry conditions.	Freely in summer, carefully in winter.	Freely in summer.
Anthurium	Flamingo plant. Tail flower. Evergreen, flowering.	Hot, humid conditions. Shade.	Cold, dry conditions. Hot or cold draughts.	Freely in summer, moderately in winter.	Sparingly.
Aphelandra	Evergreen. Flowers surrounded by coloured bracts.	Hot, humid conditions.	Cold dry conditions. Draughts.	Freely in summer, moderately in winter.	Sparingly.
Aralia (False) now Dizygotheca, q.v.					
Asparagus	*A. asparagoides*, "Smilax," *A. plumosus*, "Asparagus fern." *A. sprengeri*, fir-needle foliage. All climbers or trailers.	Moderate temperature, shade.	Heat, sunlight, drought.	Freely.	Moderately.
Aspidistra	Cast iron plant. Large green or variegated leaves. Wiry texture.	Poorish soil. Shade.	Heat. Extreme cold.	Freely in summer, moderately in winter.	Unnecessary.

NAME	DESCRIPTION	LIKES	DISLIKES	WATER	FEED
Asplenium	Fern, several varieties.	Warm, light, moist conditions. Spraying.	Cold, draughts, drought.	Freely in summer, moderately in winter.	Sparingly.
Avocado	Single or multiple stemmed tree grown from pip.	Warmth, moisture and clean leaves.	Dry conditions, draughts, extreme cold.	Moderately in summer, less in winter.	Occasionally.
Azalea	Flowering plant, pink, white, red.	Steady warmth, frequent spraying, humid conditions, constant even moisture on roots. Lime-free soil.	Cold, changing temperatures, dry roots, dry air. Lime in soil or water.	Regularly always.	Only when in flower.
Begonia rex (and other foliage Begonias)	Ornamental, coloured, "metallic," some foliage on very short stems.	Steady temperatures, some humidity, good drainage, light.	Draughts, smoke, dry conditions, hot sun.	Freely in summer, moderately in winter.	Freely in summer, rarely in winter.
Begonia (flowering) (tuberous rooted, summer)	Small, waxy, multicoloured flowers.	Warmth, humidity rich soil, good drainage, light.	Cold, draughts, hot sun.	Freely in summer, moderately in winter.	Freely when in flower.
Beloperone guttata	"Shrimp plant," pink and brown flowers.	Warm, humid, sunny conditions. Pruning.	Draughts. Cold, dry, conditions.	Freely in summer, moderately in winter.	Moderately.

146

Billbergia	Tiny trumpet flowers on long stems from leaf rosettes.	Warmth, spraying, humid conditions.	Cold, dry conditions.	Freely in summer, moderately in winter.	Seldom.
Blechnum	Fronded fern.	Continually moist soil, spraying, some light.	Drought, draughts.	Freely in summer, moderately in winter.	Seldom.
Brunfelsia	Flowering shrub.	Warm, humid conditions. Spraying.	Cold, dry conditions. Draughts.	Freely in summer, moderately in winter.	Freely in summer.
Cacti	Mainly spiny succulents.	Sunlight. Dry conditions.	Damp conditions, extreme cold. Draughts.	Moderately in summer. Seldom in winter.	Seldom, in summer.
Caladium	Patterned arrow shaped leaves.	Shady, warm conditions.	Draughts, hot sun.	Moderately in spring, freely in summer.	Regularly.
Calathea	Coloured tufted leaves.	Warm, moist, humid conditions. Shade.	Draughts, dry conditions, direct sunlight.	Freely in summer, moderately in winter.	Moderately in summer.
Calceolaria	"Slipper flower."	Light, airy, humid conditions.	Draughts, sunlight.	Moderately.	Freely in summer.
Campanula	"Bell flower."	Light, airy, cool, humid conditions.	Draughts, sunlight.	Freely in summer, moderately in winter.	Occasionally in summer.

147

NAME	DESCRIPTION	LIKES	DISLIKES	WATER	FEED
Carex	Variegated, tufted grass.	Cool, moist conditions.	Hot, dry conditions.	Freely in summer, moderately in winter.	Seldom.
Ceropegia	Purple flowered, trailing.	Warm, light, dryish conditions.	Cold, wet.	Moderately in summer, seldom in winter.	Seldom.
Chamaerops	Large palm, fan-shaped leaves.	Cool, light, airy conditions.	Hot, humid conditions.	Freely in summer, moderately in winter.	Moderately in summer.
Chlorophytum	Long, green or variegated leaves. Grasslike. Flowers on tall stems.	Normal living conditions.	Draughts, over-watering.	Freely in summer, moderately in winter.	Freely in summer.
Cineraria	Vivid, showy flowers.	Cool, light, moist, airy conditions.	Draughts, dryness.	Freely when in flower.	Freely before and during flowering.
Cissus	Kangaroo vine.	Normal living conditions. Static position.	Draughts, over-watering, moving, hot sun.	Moderately.	Moderately in summer.
Clerodendron	Flowering vine.	Warm, light, humid conditions.	Draughts, cold.	Freely in summer, seldom in winter.	Freely in summer.
Clivia	Kaffir Lily.	Warm, light, humid conditions.	Cold, draughts.	Freely in summer, seldom in winter.	Freely in summer.

Cobaea scandens	"Cups and saucers." Climbing vine.	Warm, light, humid conditions.	Cold, dark, dry conditions. Draughts.	Freely in summer, moderately in winter.	Freely in summer.
Codiaeum	Croton. Vivid coloured leaves.	Warm, light, humid conditions.	Draughts, cold, direct sunlight.	Freely in summer, moderately in winter.	Freely in summer, seldom in winter.
Coleus	Brightly coloured leaves. Soft.	Light, warmth, moisture.	Dark, cold, dry conditions.	Freely in summer, moderately in winter.	Seldom.
Crassula	Succulents.	Cool, sunny, dryish conditions.	Damp, darkness.	Moderately in summer, seldom in winter.	Seldom.
Cyclamen	Gorgeous flowers.	Warm, humid conditions. Light.	Dry, cold, draughty conditions.	Rarely in summer, freely in winter.	Moderately in autumn and winter.
Cyperus	"Umbrella plant."	Warm, moist conditions.	Cold, dryness, draughts.	Freely always.	Seldom but regularly.
Cytisus canariensis	Genista.	Cool, light, airy, moist conditions.	Dark, dry, conditions. Draughts.	Freely.	Moderately.
Dieffenbachia	"Dumb Cane." Sword-like leaves.	Warm, moist, humid, shady conditions. Spraying.	Dry, cold, conditions. Direct sunlight.	Frequently.	Moderately.
Dioscorea	Yam. Climbing plant.	Warm, sunny, airy conditions.	Cold, wet.	Moderately.	Moderately.

NAME	DESCRIPTION	LIKES	DISLIKES	WATER	FEED
Dizygotheca	"Aralia."	Warm, light conditions.	Cold, draughts, dark.	Carefully.	Freely.
Dracaena	Long, narrow, coloured leaves.	Warm, moist, light, airy conditions.	Cold, dry, dark, draughts.	Freely.	Seldom.
Elettaria cardamomum	Bamboo-like, with shorter, broader leaves.	Shady, moist, warm conditions.	Dry, cold, draughty conditions.	Freely in summer, less in winter.	Freely in summer.
Eranthemum	Ornamental foliage.	Warm, moist, light conditions.	Cold, dry conditions.	Freely in summer, moderately in winter.	Moderately.
Erica	Shrubby, flowering plant. "Heather."	Cool conditions, overhead spray. Pruning to 1"–2" of base after flowering.	Draughts and stuffy atmospheres.	Freely with rain water. Do not allow to dry out but do not water-log.	Regularly with soot water.
Euphorbia	"Crown of Thorns." Spiny plant with pale green leaves, salmon coloured flowers.	Sunny position and warm atmosphere.	Draughts and wet conditions. Too much moving.	Sparingly in winter. Carefully in summer.	Regularly in summer.

Name	Description	Likes	Dislikes	Watering	Spraying
Fatshedera lizei	Cross between fatsia and hedera. Has large 5 pointed leaves.	A shady position, fairly warm conditions.	Hot sun.	Moderately Sept.–April. Freely after.	Freely in summer. Not in winter.
Fatsia	Lobed, glossy, dark green leaves borne on a trunk.	Cool, shady position, rich soil.	Bright sun, draughts of hot or cold air.	Freely.	Regularly.
Ficus benjamina	Shrubby with long hanging leaves.	Rich soil, warmth, shady situation.	Draughts, dry conditions.	Moderately.	Seldom.
Ficus decora and F. elastica	"India Rubber plant." Large, shiny, oval leaves.	Semi shade, overhead spray, leaves cleaned.	Draughts, chlorinated water, drying out.	Freely.	Regularly.
Ficus lyrata	"Fiddle Leaf Fig." Large leaves narrow at base and broad tipped.	Warmth in winter. Regular dusting of leaves with damp cloth.	Fluctuating temperatures. Cold, chlorinated water.	Freely.	Regularly.
Ficus pumila	Climber with small leaves.	Shady position and moist atmosphere, frequent overhead spraying.	Sunny, dry conditions, draughts.	Frequently.	Regularly.
Fittonia	Small, veined, oval leaves.	Warm, humid, conditions with good drainage.	Draughts, dry conditions.	Frequently.	During summer.

151

NAME	DESCRIPTION	LIKES	DISLIKES	WATER	FEED
Geranium	See Pelargonium.				
Gloxinia	Syn. Sinningia. Large showy flowers.	Sunny position.	Draughts, cold, damp atmosphere.	Freely from Feb. to after flowering, gradually withhold till foliage dies.	Regularly when flowering.
Grevillea robusta	"Silk Oak." Fern-like, silvery leaves.	Cool and fairly light position.	Dry conditions.	Freely in summer.	Regularly during summer.
Hedera canariensis and vars	Variegated ivy. Climber with large leaves.	Warm, shady conditions. Overhead spraying.	Dry, sunny conditions.	Freely but carefully.	Regularly in summer.
Hedera helix and vars	Ivy. Many attractive varieties.	Cool, shady conditions, overhead spraying.	Dry, sunny conditions.	Freely but carefully.	Regularly in summer.
Hedera ravenholst	Large, glossy leaved climbing ivy.	Constant temperature, cool conditions.	Heat, over-watering.	Moderately.	Moderately.
Helxine	"Baby's Tears." Bright green creeper.	Shady position.	Dry atmosphere.	Water freely. It likes to paddle.	Seldom.

Name	Description	Position	Avoid	Watering	
Hoya	"Wax flower." Climber with dark glossy leaves and wax-like pendulous flowers.	Semi-shady position, good drainage, warm, humid atmosphere. Support to grow up.	Dry atmosphere.	Freely March to Sept., less during winter.	During summer.
Hydrangea	Shrubby, flowering plant.	Acid soil, light position.	Draughts, dry air.	Freely. A very thirsty plant.	Freely.
Impatiens	Fleshy plant with bright red flowers.	Sunny, warm, moist conditions.	Cold draughts.	Freely, likes to paddle in summer. Sparingly in winter.	Regularly.
Ipomaea	Annual climber with lovely flowers.	Sunny position. Support to climb up.	Shady and cold rooms.	Freely.	Freely.
Kalanchoe	Succulent with fragrant flowers.	Sunny position. Pruning after flowering.	Cold and shady rooms.	Freely in summer. Moderately in winter.	In summer.
Maranta	"Prayer Plant." Beautifully marked oblong leaves.	Shady conditions. Moist, warm, atmosphere.	Draughts and bright sun.	Freely during March–Dec. Less during winter.	Regularly during summer.
Monstera	Large, perforated leaves.	Shady position, free root run.	Draughts, fluctuating temperatures.	Freely but allow to dry out between waterings.	During growing period.

NAME	DESCRIPTION	LIKES	DISLIKES	WATER	FEED
Muehlenbeckia	Climber with wiry stems.	Sunny position.	Draughts, cold.	Sparingly.	Seldom.
Neanthe bella	A miniature palm.	Shady position, moist atmosphere, regular sponging and an annual top-dressing.	Draughts, dry atmosphere.	Freely in summer. Sparingly in winter.	During summer.
Nephrolepis	Feathery fern.	Moist, shady conditions.	Draughts, hot sun and dry atmosphere.	Freely, likes to paddle.	Regularly.
Nephthytis	See Syngonium				
Orchids	Showy, exotic plants.	Light, warm, moist conditions. Light overhead spray in summer.	Hot sun, draughts.	Carefully.	Regularly.
Palms	Large, showy plants.	Damp, shady conditions, regular sponging.	Dry atmosphere.	Freely in summer. Moderately in winter.	During summer.
Pandanus	Narrow strap-like leaves.	Moist, sunny position. Occasional overhead spray.	Cold, draughts, dry atmosphere.	Freely in summer.	During summer.

Pelargoniums	Brilliant flowers and colourful foliage.	Sunny position, good drainage. Remove leaves and flowers as they fade.	Moist conditions, gas.	Freely in summer. Sparingly in winter.	Regularly during flowering.
Pellionia	Attractively coloured stems.	Warm, shady conditions.	Wet roots, cold, draughts.	Moderately winter freely in summer.	Seldom.
Peperomia	Bushy, fleshy leaved plants, long green flowers.	Warm, moist conditions. Light position.	Draughts, too hot and dry atmosphere, bright sunlight, very cold water.	Sparingly.	During summer.
Phoenix	"Date Palm."	Cool, airy conditions.	Hot, dry atmosphere, draughts.	Freely in summer. Moderately in winter.	During summer.
Philodendron	Climber with heart shaped, large irregular, arrow-head or very deep cut leaves. Many varieties.	Shady position, warm humid conditions. Support of bark or mossy branch.	Draughts.	Freely.	Regularly.
Philodendron bipinnatifidum	Large, irregular leaves.	Warm, humid conditions, shady position.	Draughts.	Freely.	Regularly.

155

NAME	DESCRIPTION	LIKES	DISLIKES	WATER	FEED
Pilea	Oval leaves embossed with white markings.	Warm, moist, shady conditions.	Dry atmosphere, draughts.	Freely.	Regularly.
Pittosporum	Small light green leaves.	Sunny, airy conditions. Occasional syringe.	Draughts, cold.	Moderately Sept. April. Freely afterwards.	Summer.
Platycerium	"Stag's Horn" fern.	Light, warm conditions. Weekly spray.	Draughts, hot sun.	Freely when leaves begin to droop.	Regularly.
Plectranthus	Fleshy, heart shaped leaves.	Sunny, light position, some warmth.	Hot sun, draughts.	Freely in summer. Moderately in winter.	Regularly when established.
Primula	Attractive flowering plants.	Light, cool conditions.	Hot sun, draughts.	Freely.	Regularly until flower buds show colour.
Primula sinensis	Not so easy to keep.	Warm, sunny conditions.	Cold, dry, draughts.	Freely.	Freely.
Pteris	Very easy fern.	Shady position.	Draughts and direct sun.	Freely.	Sparingly.

Rhoeo discolor	Rosettes of long narrow leaves with purple undersides.	Warm, shady position.	Full sunshine.	Freely.	Regularly during flowering period.
Rhoicissus	Climber with small dark green leaves.	Cool, airy conditions but warm in winter.	Draughts.	Freely.	During summer.
Ricinus	"Castor Oil plant." With burnished bronze leaves.	Shady conditions.	Draughts, dry, hot air.	Moderately.	Occasionally.
Rochea	Fleshy plant with vivid cerise flowers.	Sunny window but fairly cool and moist conditions.	Hot, dry atmosphere.	Freely in summer. Moderately otherwise.	During summer.
Saintpaulia	Small hairy leaved plants with violet-like flowers.	Very warm, moist conditions but shady.	Draughts, gas, cold water, fluctuating atmospheres.	Freely in summer. Moderately afterwards. Always from below.	Regularly during flowering.
Sansevieria	"Mother-in-Law's Tongue." Long sword-like leaves of dark green mottled with yellow.	Sunny, dry conditions.	Too much water.	Sparingly.	Summer.

157

NAME	DESCRIPTION	LIKES	DISLIKES	WATER	FEED
Saxifraga	Reddish leaves and masses of small pink flowers. Produces numerous runners.	Cool, shady conditions.	Too much sun.	Freely in summer.	During flowering period.
Scindapsus	Yellow streaked, heart shaped leaves.	Support of bark or mossy branch. Syringe regularly, warmth.	Direct sun, draughts, handling.	Copiously March–Oct. Moderately other times.	Regularly.
Sedum	Small dainty leaves borne in threes up arching stems, insignificant flowers.	Warm, dry conditions.	Wet feet, cold, draughts.	Freely in summer. Seldom in winter.	Occasionally in summer.
Solanum	Shrubby plant with orange or yellow berries.	Cool, airy, light conditions. Daily overhead spraying.	Dry conditions, draughts hot air.	Carefully and regularly.	Twice weekly when in berry.
Sparmannia	"African hemp," furry leaves.	Light, warm, moist conditions.	Draughts and dry conditions. Direct sun.	Copiously in summer, moderately afterwards.	Summer.
Spathiphyllum	Long, dark leaves. Attractive white flowers.	Shady, moist conditions and steady temperature.	Draughts and too much sun.	Freely.	Summer regularly.

Syngonium	"Goose Foot." Lobed leaves like a goose foot.	Shady, humid, conditions. Support of bark or mossy branch.	Draughts, dry atmosphere.	Freely.	Regularly.
Tetrastigma	Climber with glossy leaves above and brown below like a horse chestnut.	Shady position, constant temperatures and conditions.	Draughts and overwatering.	Sparingly.	Regularly.
Tolmiea	"Pick-a-back plant." Light green hairy leaves producing new plants on lower leaves.	Fairly shady conditions.	Hot, dry atmosphere.	Copiously.	Moderately.
Tradescantia	"Wandering Jew." Attractively coloured oval leaves borne in pairs up fleshy stems.	Warm, light conditions.	Cold.	Freely in summer. Moderately in winter.	Regularly.
Zebrina	Dark green or wine leaves with silvery streaks.	Light, warm conditions.	Cold.	Freely in summer. Moderately in winter.	Regularly.